Mometrix
TEST PREPARATION

I0878903

Florida

Grade 5 Science Test Prep Guide

DEAR FUTURE EXAM SUCCESS STORY

First of all, **THANK YOU** for purchasing Mometrix study materials!

Second, congratulations! You are one of the few determined test-takers who are committed to doing whatever it takes to excel on your exam. **You have come to the right place.** We developed these study materials with one goal in mind: to deliver you the information you need in a format that's concise and easy to use.

In addition to optimizing your guide for the content of the test, we've outlined our recommended steps for breaking down the preparation process into small, attainable goals so you can make sure you stay on track.

We've also analyzed the entire test-taking process, identifying the most common pitfalls and showing how you can overcome them and be ready for any curveball the test throws you.

Standardized testing is one of the biggest obstacles on your road to success, which only increases the importance of doing well in the high-pressure, high-stakes environment of test day. Your results on this test could have a significant impact on your future, and this guide provides the information and practical advice to help you achieve your full potential on test day.

Your success is our success

We would love to hear from you! If you would like to share the story of your exam success or if you have any questions or comments in regard to our products, please contact us at **800-673-8175** or **support@mometrix.com**.

Thanks again for your business and we wish you continued success!

Sincerely,
The Mometrix Test Preparation Team

Written and edited by the Mometrix Exam Secrets Test Prep Team
Printed in the United States of America

TABLE OF CONTENTS

Introduction

Thank you for purchasing this resource! You have made the choice to prepare yourself for a test that could have a huge impact on your future, and this guide is designed to help you be fully ready for test day. Obviously, it's important to have a solid understanding of the test material, but you also need to be prepared for the unique environment and stressors of the test, so that you can perform to the best of your abilities.

For this purpose, the first section that appears in this guide is the **Secret Keys**. We've devoted countless hours to meticulously researching what works and what doesn't, and we've boiled down our findings to the five most impactful steps you can take to improve your performance on the test. We start at the beginning with study planning and move through the preparation process, all the way to the testing strategies that will help you get the most out of what you know when you're finally sitting in front of the test.

We recommend that you start preparing for your test as far in advance as possible. However, if you've bought this guide as a last-minute study resource and only have a few days before your test, we recommend that you skip over the first two Secret Keys since they address a long-term study plan.

If you struggle with **test anxiety**, we strongly encourage you to check out our recommendations for how you can overcome it. Test anxiety is a formidable foe, but it can be beaten, and we want to make sure you have the tools you need to defeat it.

Secret Key #1 – Plan Big, Study Small

There's a lot riding on your performance. If you want to ace this test, you're going to need to keep your skills sharp and the material fresh in your mind. You need a plan that lets you review everything you need to know while still fitting in your schedule. We'll break this strategy down into three categories.

Information Organization

Start with the information you already have: the official test outline. From this, you can make a complete list of all the concepts you need to cover before the test. Organize these concepts into groups that can be studied together, and create a list of any related vocabulary you need to learn so you can brush up on any difficult terms. You'll want to keep this vocabulary list handy once you actually start studying since you may need to add to it along the way.

Time Management

Once you have your set of study concepts, decide how to spread them out over the time you have left before the test. Break your study plan into small, clear goals so you have a manageable task for each day and know exactly what you're doing. Then just focus on one small step at a time. When you manage your time this way, you don't need to spend hours at a time studying. Studying a small block of content for a short period each day helps you retain information better and avoid stressing over how much you have left to do. You can relax knowing that you have a plan to cover everything in time. In order for this strategy to be effective though, you have to start studying early and stick to your schedule. Avoid the exhaustion and futility that comes from last-minute cramming!

Study Environment

The environment you study in has a big impact on your learning. Studying in a coffee shop, while probably more enjoyable, is not likely to be as fruitful as studying in a quiet room. It's important to keep distractions to a minimum. You're only planning to study for a short block of time, so make the most of it. Don't pause to check your phone or get up to find a snack. It's also important to **avoid multitasking**. Research has consistently shown that multitasking will make your studying dramatically less effective. Your study area should also be comfortable and well-lit so you don't have the distraction of straining your eyes or sitting on an uncomfortable chair.

The time of day you study is also important. You want to be rested and alert. Don't wait until just before bedtime. Study when you'll be most likely to comprehend and remember. Even better, if you know what time of day your test will be, set that time aside for study. That way your brain will be used to working on that subject at that specific time and you'll have a better chance of recalling information.

Finally, it can be helpful to team up with others who are studying for the same test. Your actual studying should be done in as isolated an environment as possible, but the work of organizing the information and setting up the study plan can be divided up. In between study sessions, you can discuss with your teammates the concepts that you're all studying and quiz each other on the details. Just be sure that your teammates are as serious about the test as you are. If you find that your study time is being replaced with social time, you might need to find a new team.

Secret Key #2 – Make Your Studying Count

You're devoting a lot of time and effort to preparing for this test, so you want to be absolutely certain it will pay off. This means doing more than just reading the content and hoping you can remember it on test day. It's important to make every minute of study count. There are two main areas you can focus on to make your studying count.

Retention

It doesn't matter how much time you study if you can't remember the material. You need to make sure you are retaining the concepts. To check your retention of the information you're learning, try recalling it at later times with minimal prompting. Try carrying around flashcards and glance at one or two from time to time or ask a friend who's also studying for the test to quiz you.

To enhance your retention, look for ways to put the information into practice so that you can apply it rather than simply recalling it. If you're using the information in practical ways, it will be much easier to remember. Similarly, it helps to solidify a concept in your mind if you're not only reading it to yourself but also explaining it to someone else. Ask a friend to let you teach them about a concept you're a little shaky on (or speak aloud to an imaginary audience if necessary). As you try to summarize, define, give examples, and answer your friend's questions, you'll understand the concepts better and they will stay with you longer. Finally, step back for a big picture view and ask yourself how each piece of information fits with the whole subject. When you link the different concepts together and see them working together as a whole, it's easier to remember the individual components.

Finally, practice showing your work on any multi-step problems, even if you're just studying. Writing out each step you take to solve a problem will help solidify the process in your mind, and you'll be more likely to remember it during the test.

Modality

Modality simply refers to the means or method by which you study. Choosing a study modality that fits your own individual learning style is crucial. No two people learn best in exactly the same way, so it's important to know your strengths and use them to your advantage.

For example, if you learn best by visualization, focus on visualizing a concept in your mind and draw an image or a diagram. Try color-coding your notes, illustrating them, or creating symbols that will trigger your mind to recall a learned concept. If you learn best by hearing or discussing information, find a study partner who learns the same way or read aloud to yourself. Think about how to put the information in your own words. Imagine that you are giving a lecture on the topic and record yourself so you can listen to it later.

For any learning style, flashcards can be helpful. Organize the information so you can take advantage of spare moments to review. Underline key words or phrases. Use different colors for different categories. Mnemonic devices (such as creating a short list in which every item starts with the same letter) can also help with retention. Find what works best for you and use it to store the information in your mind most effectively and easily.

Secret Key #3 – Practice the Right Way

Your success on test day depends not only on how many hours you put into preparing, but also on whether you prepared the right way. It's good to check along the way to see if your studying is paying off. One of the most effective ways to do this is by taking practice tests to evaluate your progress. Practice tests are useful because they show exactly where you need to improve. Every time you take a practice test, pay special attention to these three groups of questions:

- The questions you got wrong
- The questions you had to guess on, even if you guessed right
- The questions you found difficult or slow to work through

This will show you exactly what your weak areas are, and where you need to devote more study time. Ask yourself why each of these questions gave you trouble. Was it because you didn't understand the material? Was it because you didn't remember the vocabulary? Do you need more repetitions on this type of question to build speed and confidence? Dig into those questions and figure out how you can strengthen your weak areas as you go back to review the material.

Additionally, many practice tests have a section explaining the answer choices. It can be tempting to read the explanation and think that you now have a good understanding of the concept. However, an explanation likely only covers part of the question's broader context. Even if the explanation makes perfect sense, **go back and investigate** every concept related to the question until you're positive you have a thorough understanding.

As you go along, keep in mind that the practice test is just that: practice. Memorizing these questions and answers will not be very helpful on the actual test because it is unlikely to have any of the same exact questions. If you only know the right answers to the sample questions, you won't be prepared for the real thing. **Study the concepts** until you understand them fully, and then you'll be able to answer any question that shows up on the test.

It's important to wait on the practice tests until you're ready. If you take a test on your first day of study, you may be overwhelmed by the amount of material covered and how much you need to learn. Work up to it gradually.

On test day, you'll need to be prepared for answering questions, managing your time, and using the test-taking strategies you've learned. It's a lot to balance, like a mental marathon that will have a big impact on your future. Like training for a marathon, you'll need to start slowly and work your way up. When test day arrives, you'll be ready.

Start with the strategies you've read in the first two Secret Keys—plan your course and study in the way that works best for you. If you have time, consider using multiple study resources to get different approaches to the same concepts. It can be helpful to see difficult concepts from more than one angle. Then find a good source for practice tests. Many times, the test website will suggest potential study resources or provide sample tests.

Practice Test Strategy

If you're able to find at least three practice tests, we recommend this strategy:

Untimed and Open-Book Practice

Take the first test with no time constraints and with your notes and study guide handy. Take your time and focus on applying the strategies you've learned.

Timed and Open-Book Practice

Take the second practice test open-book as well, but set a timer and practice pacing yourself to finish in time.

Timed and Closed-Book Practice

Take any other practice tests as if it were test day. Set a timer and put away your study materials. Sit at a table or desk in a quiet room, imagine yourself at the testing center, and answer questions as quickly and accurately as possible.

Keep repeating timed and closed-book tests on a regular basis until you run out of practice tests or it's time for the actual test. Your mind will be ready for the schedule and stress of test day, and you'll be able to focus on recalling the material you've learned.

Secret Key #4 – Pace Yourself

Once you're fully prepared for the material on the test, your biggest challenge on test day will be managing your time. Just knowing that the clock is ticking can make you panic even if you have plenty of time left. Work on pacing yourself so you can build confidence against the time constraints of the exam. Pacing is a difficult skill to master, especially in a high-pressure environment, so **practice is vital**.

Set time expectations for your pace based on how much time is available. For example, if a section has 60 questions and the time limit is 30 minutes, you know you have to average 30 seconds or less per question in order to answer them all. Although 30 seconds is the hard limit, set 25 seconds per question as your goal, so you reserve extra time to spend on harder questions. When you budget extra time for the harder questions, you no longer have any reason to stress when those questions take longer to answer.

Don't let this time expectation distract you from working through the test at a calm, steady pace, but keep it in mind so you don't spend too much time on any one question. Recognize that taking extra time on one question you don't understand may keep you from answering two that you do understand later in the test. If your time limit for a question is up and you're still not sure of the answer, mark it and move on, and come back to it later if the time and the test format allow. If the testing format doesn't allow you to return to earlier questions, just make an educated guess; then put it out of your mind and move on.

On the easier questions, be careful not to rush. It may seem wise to hurry through them so you have more time for the challenging ones, but it's not worth missing one if you know the concept and just didn't take the time to read the question fully. Work efficiently but make sure you understand the question and have looked at all of the answer choices, since more than one may seem right at first.

Even if you're paying attention to the time, you may find yourself a little behind at some point. You should speed up to get back on track, but do so wisely. Don't panic; just take a few seconds less on each question until you're caught up. Don't guess without thinking, but do look through the answer choices and eliminate any you know are wrong. If you can get down to two choices, it is often worthwhile to guess from those. Once you've chosen an answer, move on and don't dwell on any that you skipped or had to hurry through. If a question was taking too long, chances are it was one of the harder ones, so you weren't as likely to get it right anyway.

On the other hand, if you find yourself getting ahead of schedule, it may be beneficial to slow down a little. The more quickly you work, the more likely you are to make a careless mistake that will affect your score. You've budgeted time for each question, so don't be afraid to spend that time. Practice an efficient but careful pace to get the most out of the time you have.

Secret Key #5 – Have a Plan for Guessing

When you're taking the test, you may find yourself stuck on a question. Some of the answer choices seem better than others, but you don't see the one answer choice that is obviously correct. What do you do?

The scenario described above is very common, yet most test takers have not effectively prepared for it. Developing and practicing a plan for guessing may be one of the single most effective uses of your time as you get ready for the exam.

In developing your plan for guessing, there are three questions to address:

- When should you start the guessing process?
- How should you narrow down the choices?
- Which answer should you choose?

When to Start the Guessing Process

Unless your plan for guessing is to select C every time (which, despite its merits, is not what we recommend), you need to leave yourself enough time to apply your answer elimination strategies. Since you have a limited amount of time for each question, that means that if you're going to give yourself the best shot at guessing correctly, you have to decide quickly whether or not you will guess.

Of course, the best-case scenario is that you don't have to guess at all, so first, see if you can answer the question based on your knowledge of the subject and basic reasoning skills. Focus on the key words in the question and try to jog your memory of related topics. Give yourself a chance to bring the knowledge to mind, but once you realize that you don't have (or you can't access) the knowledge you need to answer the question, it's time to start the guessing process.

It's almost always better to start the guessing process too early than too late. It only takes a few seconds to remember something and answer the question from knowledge. Carefully eliminating wrong answer choices takes longer. Plus, going through the process of eliminating answer choices can actually help jog your memory.

Summary: Start the guessing process as soon as you decide that you can't answer the question based on your knowledge.

How to Narrow Down the Choices

The next chapter in this book (**Test-Taking Strategies**) includes a wide range of strategies for how to approach questions and how to look for answer choices to eliminate. You will definitely want to read those carefully, practice them, and figure out which ones work best for you. Here though, we're going to address a mindset rather than a particular strategy.

Your odds of guessing an answer correctly depend on how many options you are choosing from.

Number of options left	5	4	3	2	1
Odds of guessing correctly	20%	25%	33%	50%	100%

You can see from this chart just how valuable it is to be able to eliminate incorrect answers and make an educated guess, but there are two things that many test takers do that cause them to miss out on the benefits of guessing:

- Accidentally eliminating the correct answer
- Selecting an answer based on an impression

We'll look at the first one here, and the second one in the next section.

To avoid accidentally eliminating the correct answer, we recommend a thought exercise called **the $5 challenge**. In this challenge, you only eliminate an answer choice from contention if you are willing to bet $5 on it being wrong. Why $5? Five dollars is a small but not insignificant amount of money. It's an amount you could afford to lose but wouldn't want to throw away. And while losing $5 once might not hurt too much, doing it twenty times will set you back $100. In the same way, each small decision you make—eliminating a choice here, guessing on a question there—won't by itself impact your score very much, but when you put them all together, they can make a big difference. By holding each answer choice elimination decision to a higher standard, you can reduce the risk of accidentally eliminating the correct answer.

The $5 challenge can also be applied in a positive sense: If you are willing to bet $5 that an answer choice *is* correct, go ahead and mark it as correct.

Summary: Only eliminate an answer choice if you are willing to bet $5 that it is wrong.

Which Answer to Choose

You're taking the test. You've run into a hard question and decided you'll have to guess. You've eliminated all the answer choices you're willing to bet $5 on. Now you have to pick an answer. Why do we even need to talk about this? Why can't you just pick whichever one you feel like when the time comes?

The answer to these questions is that if you don't come into the test with a plan, you'll rely on your impression to select an answer choice, and if you do that, you risk falling into a trap. The test writers know that everyone who takes their test will be guessing on some of the questions, so they intentionally write wrong answer choices to seem plausible. You still have to pick an answer though, and if the wrong answer choices are designed to look right, how can you ever be sure that you're not falling for their trap? The best solution we've found to this dilemma is to take the decision out of your hands entirely. Here is the process we recommend:

Once you've eliminated any choices that you are confident (willing to bet $5) are wrong, select the first remaining choice as your answer.

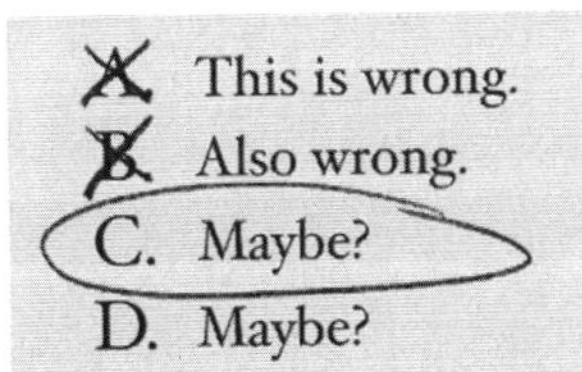

Whether you choose to select the first remaining choice, the second, or the last, the important thing is that you use some preselected standard. Using this approach guarantees that you will not be enticed into selecting an answer choice that looks right, because you are not basing your decision on how the answer choices look.

This is not meant to make you question your knowledge. Instead, it is to help you recognize the difference between your knowledge and your impressions. There's a huge difference between thinking an answer is right because of what you know, and thinking an answer is right because it looks or sounds like it should be right.

Summary: To ensure that your selection is appropriately random, make a predetermined selection from among all answer choices you have not eliminated.

Test-Taking Strategies

This section contains a list of test-taking strategies that you may find helpful as you work through the test. By taking what you know and applying logical thought, you can maximize your chances of answering any question correctly!

It is very important to realize that every question is different and every person is different: no single strategy will work on every question, and no single strategy will work for every person. That's why we've included all of them here, so you can try them out and determine which ones work best for different types of questions and which ones work best for you.

Question Strategies

✓ READ CAREFULLY

Read the question and the answer choices carefully. Don't miss the question because you misread the terms. You have plenty of time to read each question thoroughly and make sure you understand what is being asked. Yet a happy medium must be attained, so don't waste too much time. You must read carefully and efficiently.

✓ CONTEXTUAL CLUES

Look for contextual clues. If the question includes a word you are not familiar with, look at the immediate context for some indication of what the word might mean. Contextual clues can often give you all the information you need to decipher the meaning of an unfamiliar word. Even if you can't determine the meaning, you may be able to narrow down the possibilities enough to make a solid guess at the answer to the question.

✓ PREFIXES

If you're having trouble with a word in the question or answer choices, try dissecting it. Take advantage of every clue that the word might include. Prefixes can be a huge help. Usually, they allow you to determine a basic meaning. *Pre-* means before, *post-* means after, *pro-* is positive, *de-* is negative. From prefixes, you can get an idea of the general meaning of the word and try to put it into context.

✓ HEDGE WORDS

Watch out for critical hedge words, such as *likely, may, can, often, almost, mostly, usually, generally, rarely,* and *sometimes.* Question writers insert these hedge phrases to cover every possibility. Often an answer choice will be wrong simply because it leaves no room for exception. Be on guard for answer choices that have definitive words such as *exactly* and *always.*

✓ SWITCHBACK WORDS

Stay alert for *switchbacks.* These are the words and phrases frequently used to alert you to shifts in thought. The most common switchback words are *but, although,* and *however.* Others include *nevertheless, on the other hand, even though, while, in spite of, despite,* and *regardless of.* Switchback words are important to catch because they can change the direction of the question or an answer choice.

✓ Face Value

When in doubt, use common sense. Accept the situation in the problem at face value. Don't read too much into it. These problems will not require you to make wild assumptions. If you have to go beyond creativity and warp time or space in order to have an answer choice fit the question, then you should move on and consider the other answer choices. These are normal problems rooted in reality. The applicable relationship or explanation may not be readily apparent, but it is there for you to figure out. Use your common sense to interpret anything that isn't clear.

Answer Choice Strategies

✓ Answer Selection

The most thorough way to pick an answer choice is to identify and eliminate wrong answers until only one is left, then confirm it is the correct answer. Sometimes an answer choice may immediately seem right, but be careful. The test writers will usually put more than one reasonable answer choice on each question, so take a second to read all of them and make sure that the other choices are not equally obvious. As long as you have time left, it is better to read every answer choice than to pick the first one that looks right without checking the others.

✓ Answer Choice Families

An answer choice family consists of two (in rare cases, three) answer choices that are very similar in construction and cannot all be true at the same time. If you see two answer choices that are direct opposites or parallels, one of them is usually the correct answer. For instance, if one answer choice says that quantity *x* increases and another either says that quantity *x* decreases (opposite) or says that quantity *y* increases (parallel), then those answer choices would fall into the same family. An answer choice that doesn't match the construction of the answer choice family is more likely to be incorrect. Most questions will not have answer choice families, but when they do appear, you should be prepared to recognize them.

✓ Eliminate Answers

Eliminate answer choices as soon as you realize they are wrong, but make sure you consider all possibilities. If you are eliminating answer choices and realize that the last one you are left with is also wrong, don't panic. Start over and consider each choice again. There may be something you missed the first time that you will realize on the second pass.

✓ Avoid Fact Traps

Don't be distracted by an answer choice that is factually true but doesn't answer the question. You are looking for the choice that answers the question. Stay focused on what the question is asking for so you don't accidentally pick an answer that is true but incorrect. Always go back to the question and make sure the answer choice you've selected actually answers the question and is not merely a true statement.

✓ Extreme Statements

In general, you should avoid answers that put forth extreme actions as standard practice or proclaim controversial ideas as established fact. An answer choice that states the "process should be used in certain situations, if..." is much more likely to be correct than one that states the "process should be discontinued completely." The first is a calm rational statement and doesn't even make a definitive, uncompromising stance, using a hedge word *if* to provide wiggle room, whereas the second choice is far more extreme.

⊘ Benchmark

As you read through the answer choices and you come across one that seems to answer the question well, mentally select that answer choice. This is not your final answer, but it's the one that will help you evaluate the other answer choices. The one that you selected is your benchmark or standard for judging each of the other answer choices. Every other answer choice must be compared to your benchmark. That choice is correct until proven otherwise by another answer choice beating it. If you find a better answer, then that one becomes your new benchmark. Once you've decided that no other choice answers the question as well as your benchmark, you have your final answer.

⊘ Predict the Answer

Before you even start looking at the answer choices, it is often best to try to predict the answer. When you come up with the answer on your own, it is easier to avoid distractions and traps because you will know exactly what to look for. The right answer choice is unlikely to be word-for-word what you came up with, but it should be a close match. Even if you are confident that you have the right answer, you should still take the time to read each option before moving on.

General Strategies

⊘ Tough Questions

If you are stumped on a problem or it appears too hard or too difficult, don't waste time. Move on! Remember though, if you can quickly check for obviously incorrect answer choices, your chances of guessing correctly are greatly improved. Before you completely give up, at least try to knock out a couple of possible answers. Eliminate what you can and then guess at the remaining answer choices before moving on.

⊘ Check Your Work

Since you will probably not know every term listed and the answer to every question, it is important that you get credit for the ones that you do know. Don't miss any questions through careless mistakes. If at all possible, try to take a second to look back over your answer selection and make sure you've selected the correct answer choice and haven't made a costly careless mistake (such as marking an answer choice that you didn't mean to mark). This quick double check should more than pay for itself in caught mistakes for the time it costs.

⊘ Pace Yourself

It's easy to be overwhelmed when you're looking at a page full of questions; your mind is confused and full of random thoughts, and the clock is ticking down faster than you would like. Calm down and maintain the pace that you have set for yourself. Especially as you get down to the last few minutes of the test, don't let the small numbers on the clock make you panic. As long as you are on track by monitoring your pace, you are guaranteed to have time for each question.

⊘ Don't Rush

It is very easy to make errors when you are in a hurry. Maintaining a fast pace in answering questions is pointless if it makes you miss questions that you would have gotten right otherwise. Test writers like to include distracting information and wrong answers that seem right. Taking a little extra time to avoid careless mistakes can make all the difference in your test score. Find a pace that allows you to be confident in the answers that you select.

⊘ KEEP MOVING

Panicking will not help you pass the test, so do your best to stay calm and keep moving. Taking deep breaths and going through the answer elimination steps you practiced can help to break through a stress barrier and keep your pace.

Final Notes

The combination of a solid foundation of content knowledge and the confidence that comes from practicing your plan for applying that knowledge is the key to maximizing your performance on test day. As your foundation of content knowledge is built up and strengthened, you'll find that the strategies included in this chapter become more and more effective in helping you quickly sift through the distractions and traps of the test to isolate the correct answer.

Now that you're preparing to move forward into the test content chapters of this book, be sure to keep your goal in mind. As you read, think about how you will be able to apply this information on the test. If you've already seen sample questions for the test and you have an idea of the question format and style, try to come up with questions of your own that you can answer based on what you're reading. This will give you valuable practice applying your knowledge in the same ways you can expect to on test day.

Good luck and good studying!

Nature of Science

Science Knowledge and Scientific Process

Scientific knowledge is knowledge about the world that we understand by observing and testing. The **scientific process** is how we try to gain scientific knowledge. The steps are to make an initial observation, create a hypothesis, test the hypothesis with an experiment, draw conclusions from the experiment, then start over with new observations.

Observations

An **observation** is something specific you notice about the world or an event. For instance, a very obvious event that takes place is if we leave milk out on the counter overnight, the milk will go bad. We observe this event by using our five senses: sight, taste, smell, touch, and sound. When milk goes bad, there are several ways it changes, including the way it looks and smells.

Asking Questions

Observations may inspire new questions. These questions can be used to form a hypothesis, which can be used to design an experiment. When trying to gain scientific knowledge, it is best to ask questions that are clear and specific, or well defined. This can make answering the question easier. When a question is not clear or is not specific, it may have several possible answers. It also may have an answer that only leads to more questions. For example, the question "what will happen if you drop an egg" is not a well-defined question. The result of dropping an egg depends on many factors, and there are many possible answers to the question. However, the question "what will happen if you drop an uncooked egg on concrete" is a well-defined question. The question is specific and clear, and it can be tested using a simple experiment.

Hypothesis

After making observations, the next step is to make an educated guess about what might happen in a certain event. This is also known as a **hypothesis**. A hypothesis about milk might be that if I keep milk above a certain temperature for a long time, it will go bad. Hypotheses need to be specific and testable so it can be determined whether they are true or false.

Experiment

The step after creating a hypothesis is to check if it is true by testing it with an **experiment**. An experiment is a type of investigation that follows a list of steps in order to find evidence that supports or does not support a hypothesis. Experiments need to include a controlled, specific situation that reveals whether or not the hypothesis is correct. Experiments need to ask questions about **facts**, rather than **opinions**. The hypothesis can help the experimenter decide what steps should be included in the experiment.

Variables

Experiments include variables. **Variables** are parts of an experiment that may be changed or kept the same during the experiment, and some variables affect others. An **independent variable** is a variable that the experimenter will change during the experiment, and a **dependent variable** is a variable that changes in response to changes to an independent variable. Independent variables are changed, and dependent variables are observed. Variables need to be controlled as much as possible to get the most specific results.

Experiments Testing One Variable

Experiments should be designed to only test the effects of one variable. This helps experimenters make sure that the cause of the experiment's results is clear and certain. To make sure that the experiment only tests one variable, the experiment should only have one independent variable. For example, the height that sunflowers would grow in different circumstances depends on many factors that could be changed by the experimenter. Sunflowers are affected by the amount of water and sunlight they receive, the soil in which they are planted, the amount of space they have to grow, and the temperature of the air around them. If more than one of these factors are independent variables, then the experimenter may not be able to tell which factor affected growth of the sunflower. If only one of these factors is an independent variable, then the experimenter will know which factor affected the sunflower, since it will be the only thing that was changed by the experimenter.

Constants and Controls

To ensure that there is only one independent variable, other factors cannot be changed by the experimenter. These factors are called **constants**. Another aspect of an experiment is the control. A **control** is an example where the independent variable is not manipulated. The group in which the independent variable was manipulated can then be compared to the control group.

Collecting Information During an Experiment

An experimenter makes observations during an experiment, writes them down, and then uses those observations to **draw conclusions**. Observations made during an experiment become **data**. Accurately **measuring** and **recording** data is necessary for an effective scientific investigation. **Accuracy** describes how close a measurement is to the true value. Not accurately measuring during an experiment may cause an experimenter to misunderstand the results of the experiment. For example, investigating how much plants grow when given different amounts of water would require the experimenter to accurately measure and record how much water each plant received and how much each plant grew daily. When an experimenter is writing and sharing the conclusion of a scientific investigation, accurate information and specific observations are needed so the experiment can be repeated and considered to be reliable.

> **Review Video: What is the Scientific Method?**
> Visit mometrix.com/academy and enter code: 191386

Observations Versus Ideas and Inferences

Scientists must keep records of their experiments and the observations they make by taking notes and drawing their observations. An observation is something a scientist experiences using their senses. Observations are not ideas or inferences. An idea is a thought that a scientist might have about an observation, but it is not the observation itself. An inference is a thought that might explain what a scientist has observed, but this, too, is different from an observation. Observations, ideas, and inferences are all important for scientific discovery, but observations are factual experiences, while ideas and inferences are thoughts that have to do with the observations.

Observations Versus Opinions

It is important for scientists to come up with explanations and opinions about their observations, but it is equally important to understand the difference between opinions and observations. An observation is something that a scientist has personally seen and/or experienced. Opinions and interpretations are thoughts the scientist has about those observations. An interpretation can explain why an observation has occurred. For example, a scientist may observe that trees lose their leaves when it gets colder. That scientist may form an opinion or interpretation that the trees are shedding their leaves to save energy during the winter.

Direct and Indirect Evidence

Evidence refers to the data and facts that **support** a hypothesis or explanation. There are different types of evidence that are used when analyzing the result of a scientific investigation:

- **Direct evidence** is any evidence that clearly supports the hypothesis or explanation and does not need any additional support. A fossil, which is the preserved remains of a past organism, is an example of direct evidence. Fossils show that certain organisms existed long ago.
- **Indirect evidence** is evidence that is used with additional evidence and inferences to support the hypothesis or explanation. For example, identifying why an animal learned a new behavior would require looking at indirect evidence. One might look at the animal's original behavior, its new behavior, and any events that occurred before the animal began to behave differently. These pieces of evidence could be used to infer a reason for the animal's adaptation, but this evidence does not clearly prove why the animal learned the new behavior.

Both types of evidence are important for supporting a hypothesis. Direct evidence can be used to prove exactly what happened, while indirect evidence can be used to make connections that will lead to a better understanding and explanation of what took place during the investigation.

Validating Explanations Through Evidence

Whenever scientists try to explain an observation, they must test their ideas to see if those ideas are correct. During an experiment, scientists will observe any changes that happen and take measurements to either support or disprove their interpretation of the first observation. Without these observations and measurements, scientists would not have enough evidence to support their ideas and, therefore, no reason for other people to believe their ideas. For example, if a scientist notices that it rains a lot in the summer, the scientist may form an opinion that summer has the rainiest months. To find out if this idea is correct, the scientist would need to measure the amount of rainfall each season by collecting rain throughout the year. The measurements of how much rain fell each season are data that will support or disprove the scientist's idea that summer has the rainiest months.

Repeating Experiments

Experiments should be **repeated** to see if the same result happens every time. For example, if you can get the same result in only three out of ten attempts, then the result is not reliable, and the experiment should be changed and tried again.

The results of an investigation that is only run once are not completely reliable. When an investigation is run the exact same way again and again and the result is the same every time, then the result is more likely to be considered reliable. If the investigation has only been completed once, or even just a few times, the results may be a result of chance or an error. When an investigation can be repeated, there is an opportunity for other discoveries to occur. An investigation may be repeated and produce different results. While those results may not be reliable, they can still lead to a new discovery or idea that can be investigated. The results of a repeated investigation may become a scientific theory, which is an explanation of an event that has become widely accepted by the science community.

Reflect

After an experiment is complete, the scientist needs to **reflect** on what happened by asking questions:

- Did the experiment answer the question?
- Was the hypothesis true or false?
- Did repeated attempts produce the same results?
- Is there anything I should change for future attempts?
- What did I learn?
- What questions can I ask now that I have learned something?

Repeat the Process

After the experiment and reflection is over, the scientist hopefully learned something and can ask new questions. These questions should be more specific, or the experiment should be improved to get better answers.

Replicability by Others

When scientists investigate their observations, they must write down or draw everything they observe, measure, and interpret from their experiments. One of the main reasons to record this information is to allow other scientists to perform the same experiment. Without detailed notes about how the experiment is set up and performed, another scientist would not have adequate instructions to re-create the experiment. It is important that other scientists perform the same experiment to find out if others can get the same results as the first scientist. If the scientists who re-creates the experiment get the same results, that further supports the first scientist's ideas. If the first scientist's results cannot be replicated, that scientist's ideas will be rejected. For example, a sick patient would not want to take a new medicine that was only tested and found safe for one person in one experiment. The patient would want the medicine to be proven to work in many tests on many people to make sure it is safe.

Other Types of Scientific Investigations

While many scientists use the scientific method to guide their research and experiments, scientists also use other methods for studying and learning. Some scientists work by observing something, asking a question about it, investigating, collecting information, trying to understand the information, and then sharing their interpretation of what the information means with others. Other kinds of scientists might ask themselves how to solve a problem, imagine the solution, make plans for a machine or system to solve the problem, build it, and then test and improve on what they made. Scientific research can also happen without using a method, but science always involves observations. Observations occur when someone notices something about the world using their senses. Scientists test their observations to understand them. Testing helps scientists develop reasons why the thing they observed happened.

Sharing Results

The result of a scientific investigation is valuable information that others may want to know. These results may help other scientists learn new information that is related to their own research and investigations. They may also help others if the information changes the way people may look at an everyday product or activity. However, results can be communicated in different ways. When the results of an experiment can be expressed using numbers, different graphs and charts can share the information in a way that emphasizes patterns and the investigator's conclusions. Lab reports are also useful when sharing the results of an investigation. A lab report includes a description of the investigation, so the reader will know which methods were used in the investigation and the results of the investigation.

Lab Reports

A **lab report** should begin with a statement describing the problem or question being investigated. It should also include the hypothesis and list the variables in the experiment. Both a list of all materials used and the detailed procedure that was followed during the investigation are important to include. These will allow other scientists to replicate the investigation. A lab report should also list the results of an investigation. Any data tables or observations that are part of the results need to be labeled correctly and include accurate measurements and calculations. Finally, a lab report should conclude with an explanation that uses the evidence that was found during the investigation to state whether the hypothesis was supported or not supported. Also, the conclusion should include a detailed summary of the data collected during the investigation, and it should describe any errors that might have occurred during the investigation.

Venn Diagrams

One helpful way of sorting out information when comparing two things is a **Venn diagram.** This tool is made by drawing two circles that overlap. It is used to display which qualities of one thing are similar or different from the qualities of another thing. In the following diagram, notice how fish and frogs are similar in some ways, but different in others.

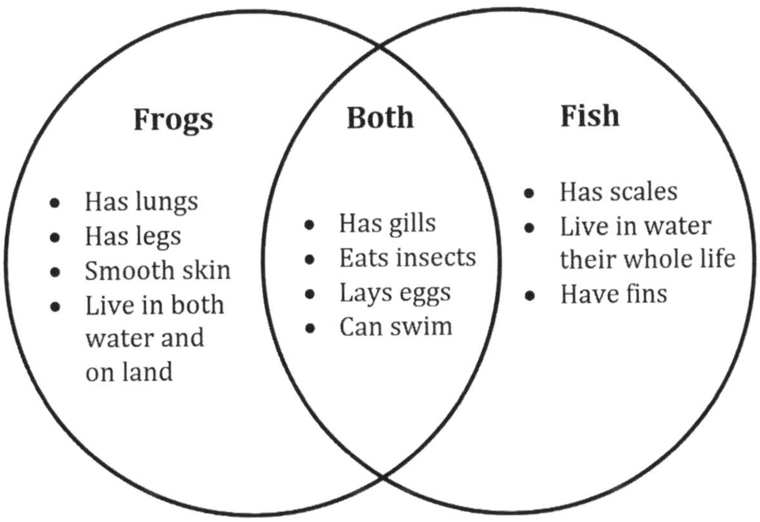

Frequency Tables

Frequency tables show how frequently each unique value appears in a set. A **relative frequency table** is one that shows the proportions of each unique value compared to the entire set. Relative frequencies are given as percentages; however, the total percent for a relative frequency table will not necessarily equal 100 percent due to rounding. An example of a frequency table with relative frequencies is below.

Favorite Color	Frequency	Relative Frequency
Blue	4	13%
Red	7	22%
Green	3	9%
Purple	6	19%
Cyan	12	38%

Circle Charts

Circle charts, also known as **pie charts**, show what portion of a whole set of data is made of a specific type of data. The circle chart is divided into sections by drawing lines to create wedges. The percentage of the circle that each wedge takes up is equal to the percentage of the whole data set that is taken up by that type of data. When complete, a circle chart often looks like a pie cut into uneven wedges. That is why it may also be called a pie chart.

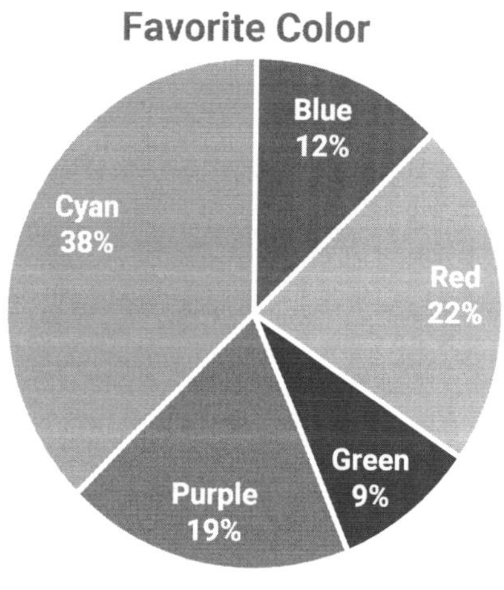

Pictographs

A **pictograph** is a graph that uses pictures or symbols to represent data. Each pictograph must have a key that defines the picture or symbol and tells what quantity each picture or symbol represents. Pictures or symbols on a pictograph are not always shown as whole pictures or symbols. In this case, the fraction of the picture or symbol shown represents the same fraction of the quantity the whole picture or symbol stands for. For example, a row with $3\frac{1}{2}$ ears of corn, where each ear of corn represents 100 stalks of corn in a field, would equal $3\frac{1}{2} \times 100 = 350$ stalks of corn in the field.

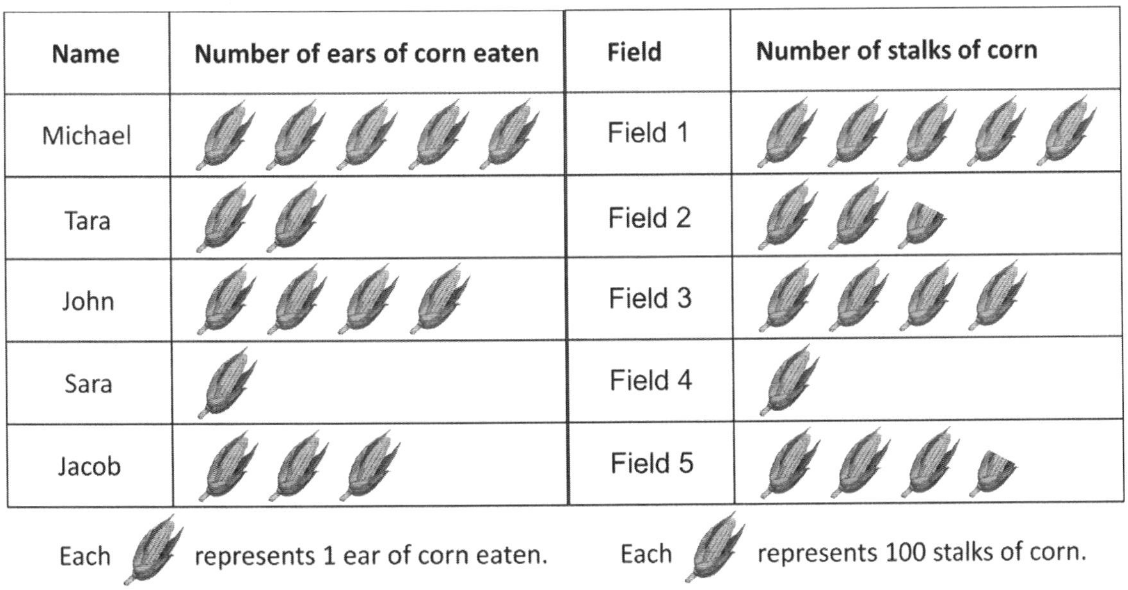

Review Video: Pictographs
Visit mometrix.com/academy and enter code: 147860

Line Graphs

Line graphs have one or more lines of varying styles (solid or broken) to show the different values for a set of data. The individual data are represented as ordered pairs, much like on a coordinate plane. In this case, the *x*- and *y*-axes represent units, such as dollars or time. The individual plotted points are joined by line segments to show whether the value of the data is increasing (line sloping upward), decreasing (line sloping downward), or staying the same (horizontal line). Multiple sets of data can be graphed on the same line graph so they can be easily compared. An example of this would be graphing test scores for different students over the same time period. The graph will show which students had the greatest increase or decrease in their scores from year to year.

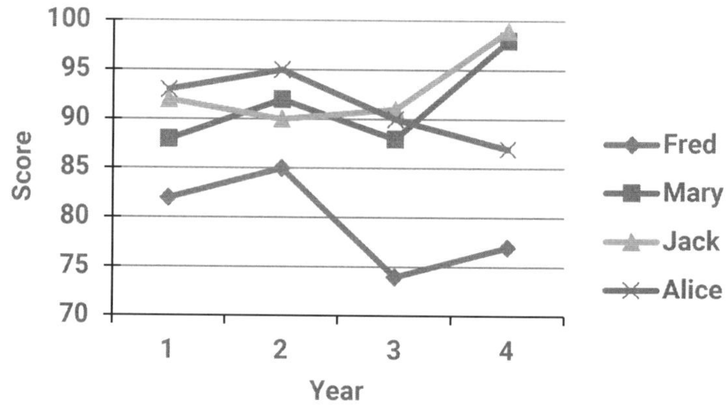

Review Video: How to Create a Line Graph
Visit mometrix.com/academy and enter code: 480147

Line Plots

A **line plot**, also known as a **dot plot**, has plotted points that are not connected by line segments. In this type of graph, the horizontal axis lists the different possible values for the data, and the vertical axis lists the number of times each value occurs. A single dot is graphed for each value to show the number of times it occurs. This graph is more closely related to a bar graph than to a line graph. Do not connect the dots in a line plot, or it will misrepresent the data.

Review Video: Line Plot
Visit mometrix.com/academy and enter code: 754610

STEM AND LEAF PLOTS

A **stem and leaf plot** is useful for depicting groups of data that fall into a range of values. Each piece of data is separated into two parts: the first, or left, part is called the stem; the second, or right, part is called the leaf. Each stem is listed in a column from smallest to largest. Each leaf that has the common stem is listed in that stem's row from smallest to largest. For example, in a set of two-digit numbers, the digit in the tens place is the stem, and the digit in the ones place is the leaf. With a stem and leaf plot, you can easily see which subset of numbers (10s, 20s, 30s, etc.) is the largest. This information is also readily available by looking at a histogram, but a stem and leaf plot also allows you to look closer and see exactly which values fall in that range. Using a sample set of test scores (82, 88, 92, 93, 85, 90, 92, 95, 74, 88, 90, 91, 78, 87, 98, 99), we can assemble a stem and leaf plot like the one below.

Test Scores

7	4	8							
8	2	5	7	8	8				
9	0	0	1	2	2	3	5	8	9

Review Video: Stem-and-Leaf Plots
Visit mometrix.com/academy and enter code: 302339

BAR GRAPHS

A **bar graph** is similar to a line plot in the way the data is organized on the graph. Bar graphs can be vertical or horizontal, but both axes must have their categories labelled for the graph to be useful. Rather than placing a single dot to mark the point of the data's value, a bar, or thick line, is drawn from zero to the exact value of the data. The value may be a number, percentage, or other numerical value. Longer bar lengths correspond to greater data values. To read a bar graph, read the labels for the axes to find the units being represented. Then, look where the bars end in relation to the scale given on the other axis and find the value of the data.

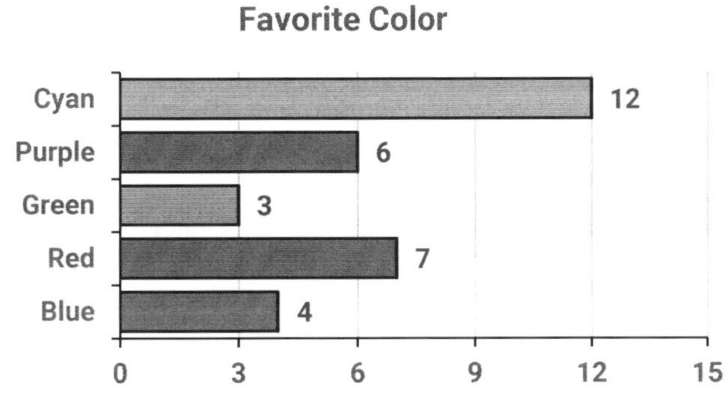

Evaluating Scientific Explanations

The results of an investigation and the conclusions that scientists make after studying data are used to create scientific explanations. **Explanations** seek to describe why natural events happen and provide new details about scientific discoveries. However, some explanations are not reliable. When new scientific explanations are made, it is important to evaluate them to see if they are reliable and possible. Important factors to think about and questions to ask when evaluating a scientific explanation are:

- **Logic:** Does the explanation make sense? Is the explanation reasonable? Does it seem possible?
- **Question or Problem:** Was the question or problem that the investigation studied well-defined? Did the investigation results answer that question?
- **Experimental methods:** Is the method used in the experiment reliable? Did the experimenter record their process? Was the experiment performed properly and carefully?
- **Tools:** Did the tools used take accurate measurements? Were the correct tools used?
- **Evidence:** Is the explanation based on direct or indirect evidence? Does the evidence support the explanation well?
- **Research:** Did the investigator use reliable, scientific resources when doing research related to the investigation or experiment?

Scientific Models

Scientists often create **models** to help express and understand scientific ideas. A model is a representation of an idea that is used to experience something that cannot be experienced directly. For instance, we cannot see and experience evaporation directly, but we can easily draw out the process of evaporation, condensation, and precipitation. Having a drawing helps us to understand the concept since we cannot experience it directly. Models can be three-dimensional, such as something you can hold, or they can be simple diagrams showing a process. For instance, a planetarium is a large model that helps someone see the size of planets and stars and how they interact. More typical models in the classroom include baking soda and vinegar volcanoes, solar system mobiles, or molecules made from foam and straws. Other models can include a diagram showing the water cycle, round objects showing the movement and location of the Sun, Moon, and Earth, or layers of different materials showing how sedimentary rocks and fossil fuels are made.

Limitations of Models

Models can be helpful for experiencing a scientific process that normally could not be observed directly, but they are limited. Models are usually used to display a very large thing in a small way, such as showing a volcano or the Earth in a way that a human can look at it and touch it. Models are also often used to express very small things or invisible things in a more observable way. Changing the size or the materials used to express something limits how similar a model can be to the real thing. For instance, if a model of the water cycle used cotton balls to show clouds, it limits our understanding of clouds. Clouds are not made of dry, solid cotton, but are made up of vapor filled with water. Volcanos made from clay that use baking soda and vinegar do not demonstrate the extreme heat or mass of volcanic materials. Similarly, a mobile of the solar system cannot express how extremely large the Sun and planets are. When using a model to understand a concept, the observer needs to be aware that they are probably only getting a clear picture of a small part of the concept, not gaining full understanding from the model.

Measurement

Tools for Measuring and Observation

Purpose	Tool
Measuring length	Rulers, meter sticks
Measuring weight or mass	Spring scales, pan balances
Measuring volume	Beakers, graduated cylinders
Measuring time	Timers, clocks
Measuring temperature	Thermometer
Recording information	Journals, notebooks
Observing animals and plants	Terrariums, aquariums, collecting nets
Observing weather	Rain gauges, wind vanes
Observing light	Prisms, mirrors
Observing magnetism	Magnets
Observing effects of heat	Hot plates
Models for understanding concepts	Sun-Earth-Moon system models, volcano models, water cycle models
Visual observation	cameras, hand lenses, microscopes
Making calculations	Calculators, computers

Metric System

The **metric system** is the accepted standard of measurement in the scientific community. **Standardization** is important because it allows the results of experiments to be compared and reproduced without the need to convert measurements. The metric system uses similar conversions between all types of measurement, including length, mass, volume, time, and temperature.

Customary and Metric (Scientific) Units of Measurement

The customary system commonly used in the United States is not based on consistent smaller units. Thus, 12 inches equal 1 foot, 3 feet equal 1 yard, and 5,280 feet equal 1 mile. The metric system used in science and in most countries is based on units of 10. Therefore, 1000 millimeters and 100 centimeters equal 1 meter, and 1,000 meters equal 1 kilometer. Most units of measurement follow the pattern of being based on units of 10, with a notable exception being temperature. The following table shows some different units.

Unit	Customary System	Metric System
Length	Inch, foot, mile	Centimeter, meter, kilometer
Mass, weight	Net weight ounce, pound	Gram, kilogram, newton
Volume	Fluid ounce, pint, quart	Milliliter, liter
Temperature	Fahrenheit degree	Celsius degree

Basic Units of Measurement

The **metric system** is generally accepted as the preferred measurement system. Having a **universal standard** allows individuals to interpret measurements more easily, regardless of where they are located. The basic units of measurement are the **meter**, which measures length; the **liter**, which measures volume; and the **gram**, which measures mass. The metric system starts with a base unit and increases or decreases in units of 10. The prefix and the base unit combined are used to indicate an amount. For example, deka- is 10 times the base unit. A decameter, or dekameter, is 10 meters; a decaliter, or dekaliter, is 10 liters; and a decagram, or dekagram, is 10 grams. The prefix hecto- refers to 100 times the base amount and kilo- is 1,000 times the base amount. The prefixes that indicate a fraction of the base unit are deci-, which is 1/10 of the base unit; centi-, which is 1/100 of the base unit; and milli-, which is 1/1000 of the base unit.

Review Video: Metric System Conversions
Visit mometrix.com/academy and enter code: 163709

Common Prefixes

The prefixes for **multiples** are as follows:

Deca or Deka	(da)	10
Hecto	(h)	100
Kilo	(k)	1,000
Mega	(M)	100,000

The prefixes for **subdivisions** are as follows:

Deci	(d)	1/10
Centi	(c)	1/100
Milli	(m)	1/1,000
Micro	(μ)	1/100,000

Fahrenheit and Celsius Temperature Scales

In the Fahrenheit scale the point where water freezes and ice melts is set at 32°, and the point where water boils and water vapor condenses is 212°. That means there is a difference of 180° between the freezing and boiling points of water. In the Celsius scale, the freezing/melting point is set at 0°and the boiling/condensation point at 100°, making this scale much easier to use.

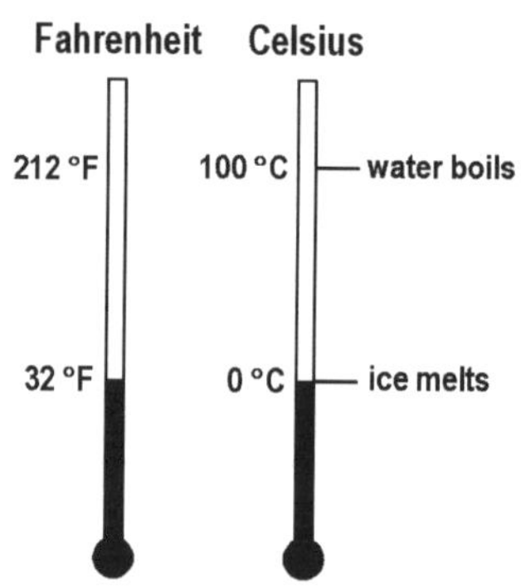

Contributions of Scientists

- **Sir Francis Bacon** – contributed many ideas that helped develop the modern scientific method.
- **Galileo Galilei**– one of the first people to use a telescope and contributed ideas about how gravity works. He also contributed the idea that the Earth revolved around the Sun, and not the other way around.
- **Leonardo da Vinci** – known for his contributions to art and to science, he was an avid inventor, designing a submarine, an armored tank, and several aircraft far before any of which were actually built.
- **Sir Isaac Newton** – best known for his contributions to physics. He described the principles of inertia and friction.
- **Louis Pasteur** – discovered bacteria, invented the process of pasteurization, and developed some of the first vaccines.
- **Thomas Edison** – invented many distinct devices, including the phonograph, improved the telephone, the lightbulb, and the kinetoscope, an early form of movie projector.
- **Albert Einstein** – studied theoretical physics with the use of mathematics and is particularly famous for his theory of relativity.

Chapter Quiz

1. A student is working on a science project and is going through each step of the scientific method. After the student conducts his or her first experiment and records the results of the experimental test, what should the student do next?

a. Communicate the results.
b. Draw a conclusion.
c. Repeat the experiment.
d. Create a hypothesis.

2. The experiment Rachel completed is outlined below to see which type of soda removes the most rust off a nail.

Step 1:	Collect 4 nails with the exact same amount of rust
Step 2:	Place 1 nail in a 20-ounce bottle of Dr. Pepper, Coke, and Sprite. Leave the final nail off to the side.
Step 3:	After 45 minutes, pour out the soda and nail.
Step 4:	Wipe each nail with a paper towel, and observe which nail changed the most from its original state.

What is the controlled group in this experiment?

a. types of soda
b. four nails
c. nail not placed in the soda
d. paper towel

3. Students are conducting an experiment to determine which laundry detergent is more effective at removing ketchup stains from a white t-shirt. The students squirted two teaspoons of ketchup on the front of three identical white shirts. They let the ketchup sit on each shirt for thirty minutes and then washed the shirt in one of the three detergents being tested. After all three shirts had been washed, the students determined that the second detergent used was the most effective at removing the ketchup stain. What is the best way to improve this experiment?

a. Students should use three different types of white shirts instead of identical ones.
b. Students should leave the ketchup on each shirt for an hour instead of just 30 minutes.
c. Students should use a different brand of ketchup on each shirt.
d. Students should repeat the exact experiment two or three more times to increase the reliability of the results.

4. Students have just completed a lab. What can they do to be sure that their results are reliable?

a. Repeat the lab again
b. Compare their data to data collected in similar experiments
c. Measure all of their results twice with two different rulers
d. Make sure that their results confirm that their hypothesis was correct

5. After completing the experiment that was assigned to the class, Sarah and Michael are unsure if their results are accurate. Which would be the best next step for them to follow?

a. Design a different experiment that would make it easier to get valid results.
b. Ask other classmates about the methods used in the experiment and compare results.
c. Start over completely and forget about the results from the first attempt.
d. Try altering the procedures slightly to make them easier to accomplish correctly.

6. After completing the same experiment, the teacher had the groups of students compare the observations they made with the observations of other groups. The groups noticed that there were small differences in the observations. Which of the following would NOT be a reason for small differences in observations?

a. Different groups completed the given procedures in slightly different ways.
b. Some groups used beakers to measure the liquids while others used small measuring cups.
c. Some groups typed their observations while others wrote them on paper.
d. Some groups weighed objects on a scale while other groups used a balance.

7. Luis and Carl place three ivy plants on the windowsill in their classroom. Every morning they water the plants. Plant one receives 50 mL of tap water, plant two receives 50 mL of distilled water, and plant 3 receives 50 mL of salt water. Every Friday, they measure the plants and record their height. The students are trying to determine which type of water will help the plant grow the fastest. Is this a systematic observation or an experiment?

a. It is a systematic observation because students are trying to answer a question.
b. It is a systematic observation because the students are giving the plants the same amount of water each morning.
c. It is an experiment because the students are recording the data each week to determine the results.
d. It is an experiment because the type of plant and amount of water are controlled conditions, and the only difference is the type of water.

8. Alexander and Elizabeth are investigating magnets. They notice that when they move magnet 1 toward the iron washer it attracts the washer from about six inches away. They notice when they move magnet 2 toward the same iron washer, it must be very close to the washer before it visibly attracts the washer. What inference can Alexander and Elizabeth make based on their observations in this experiment?

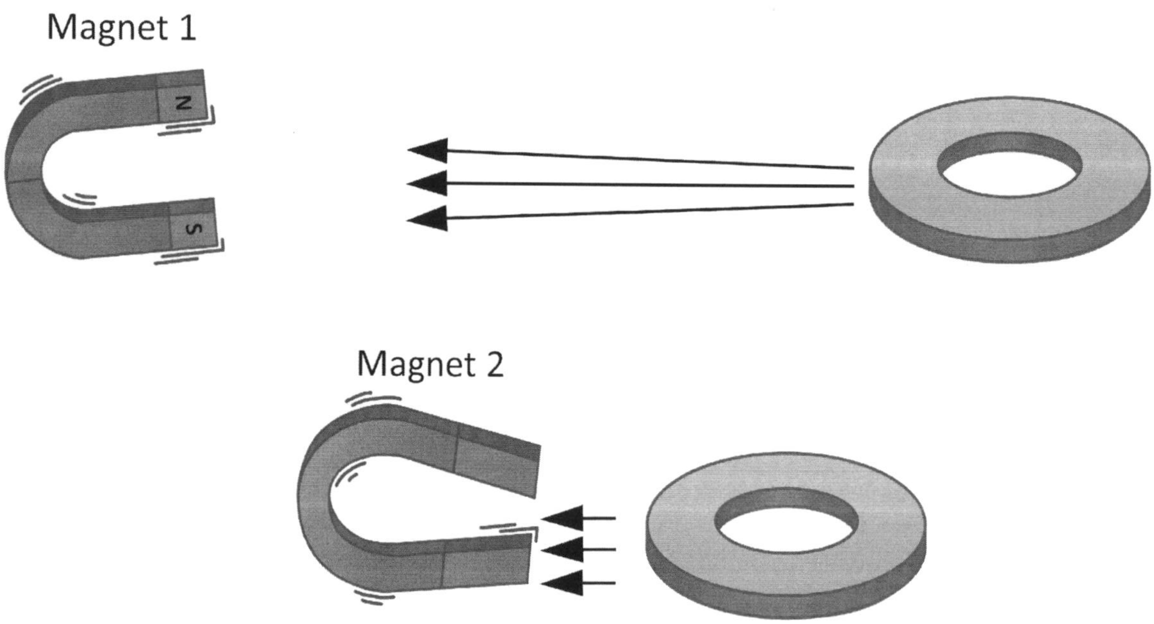

a. Magnet 1 is a stronger magnet than magnet 2.
b. Magnet 2 must be a much larger magnet than magnet 1.
c. Magnet 2 is a stronger magnet than magnet 1.
d. Magnet 2 wasn't actually magnetic.

9. Students in Mrs. Jackson's class are trying to build the sturdiest container for an egg, so that when the egg is dropped, it is protected. The students use various materials to create the container. They then climb on a ladder and drop the container with an egg inside. Some students drop from the top of the ladder, and others drop from the middle of the ladder. After dropping, students record the state of the egg. Some eggs broke, while others remained intact. What could be done to make this experiment more reliable?

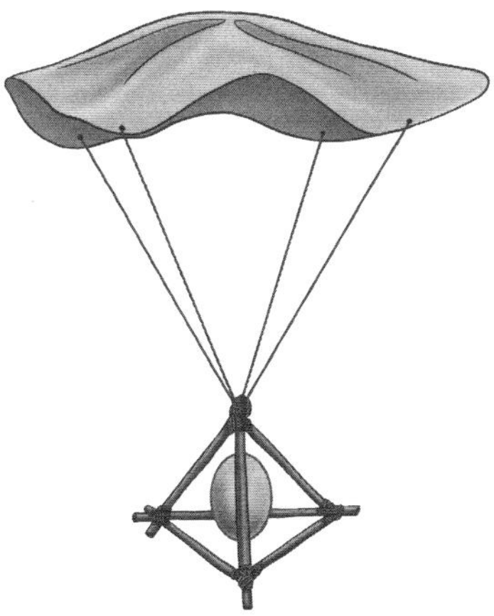

a. Students should use hard boiled eggs so there is less mess.
b. Students should drop the egg containers from the same height.
c. Students should create the exact same containers for the egg drop.
d. Students should drop their egg containers on different days.

10. Students conduct an experiment using a marble, an inclined plane, and various surfaces like felt, turf, aluminum foil, and wax paper. Students cover the inclined plane with one of the various surfaces, place the marble at the top of the inclined plane, and then raise the inclined place two inches off the ground. Finally, they record the amount of time it takes the marble to travel to the bottom of the inclined plane. They complete this experiment the exact same way with each of the different surfaces. What question are students trying to answer?

a. Which surfaces provide more friction than others?
b. How fast can a marble travel down an inclined plane?
c. Does the weight of the marble affect how fast it travels?
d. What type of marbles travel the easiest?

Chapter Quiz Answers and Explanations

1. C: Repeating the experiment validates data. Each separate experiment is called a repetition. It should be possible to replicate the results of experiments or tests. Similar data gathered from many experiments can also be used to quantify the validity of the hypothesis. Repeating the experiments allows the student to observe variation in the results. Variation in data can be caused by a variety of errors or may be evidence against the hypothesis. Answer D, Create a hypothesis, comes before experiments. Answers A, Communicate the results, and B, Draw a conclusion, occur after testing.

2. C: The controlled group in this experiment was the nail not placed in the soda because it was not changed in any way. It is the nail that the nails that were placed in the soda can be compared to when observing changes. The types of soda were the variables. The three nails placed in the soda do not represent the control group because they were given the specific treatment. The paper towel is just another material used in the experiment.

3. D: Repeating the exact experiment a few more times will increase the reliability of the results by eliminating results due to human error therefore improving the experiment. Using different types of white shirts or a different brand of ketchup adds another variable to the experiment and makes it less reliable. Leaving the ketchup on for longer changes the experiment but doesn't improve it in any way.

4. A: To be the more precise, the students could complete the lab again. In fact, all scientific laws have been developed by being tested over and over again through repetitive scientific experiment.

5. B: Sarah and Michael should talk to other classmates because scientists often ask questions and discuss the results of their experiments with other scientists to compare information and discover patterns in the results. Starting a completely different experiment would not help determine if their current experiment is valid or not and might result in the same problem they have now. Restarting the experiment and forgetting about the first attempt would not show if the first results were accurate or not. Altering the procedures will alter the results and will make them less accurate.

6. C: The way in which the observations are recorded would have no impact on differences in the observations. Slight differences in observations are commonly the result of different measuring tools and different interpretations and implementation of the procedures in the experiment.

7. D: It is an experiment since all the conditions are controlled except for one, the type of water the plants are given. This is the main difference between a systematic observation and experiment. A systematic observation may start with a question, but experiments answer questions as well. Giving the plants the same amount of water is not enough evidence to distinguish between a systematic observation and an experiment. Recording data takes place in both experiments and systematic observations.

8. A: Since magnet 1 attracted the washer at a much further distance than magnet 2, it can be inferred that magnet 1 is a stronger magnet. It is not always true that a larger magnet is a stronger magnet. However, with this reasoning it would have been inferred that magnet 2 would have been a smaller magnet, not larger. It cannot be inferred that magnet 2 was stronger since it had to be at a closer distance to the washer to attract it. Magnet 2 still attracted the iron washer, so it is still a magnet.

9. B: The experiment would be more reliable if students dropped the egg containers from the same height because this would limit the variables. Dropping them from different heights may be the reason that some broke and others did not. Using hard boiled eggs would make the experiment less messy, but not more reliable. If students created the exact same container, it would limit the findings of the experiment. Dropping the containers on different days would make the experiment less reliable because it would introduce more variables.

10. A: The students are testing different materials that provide different amounts of friction to the marble as it travels down the inclined plane. They are trying to see which surfaces have more friction than others. Students are not trying to get the marble to travel the fastest. The type of marble doesn't ever change so students are not testing the weight or type of marble.

Earth and Space Science

Components of the Universe

The universe is made up of many types of celestial objects, including stars, planets, nebulae, and galaxies, among others.

- **Stars** are giant balls of plasma that are mostly composed of helium and hydrogen. Stars have very large masses and extremely high temperatures, ranging from approximately 2,000 to 50,000 °C. There are different types of stars, and a star's type is based upon its mass, age, size, color, luminosity, and temperature.
- **Planets** are self-contained, spherical bodies that are shaped by their own gravitational force. Most planets rotate on their own axis and orbit a star. Planets can be made up of rocky material, gases, or different types of ice. They have much smaller masses and lower temperatures than stars.
- **Nebulae** are gigantic clouds of gas and dust where new stars are often born. They come in a range of shapes and sizes and are bigger than stars but smaller than galaxies. They are more diffuse and much less dense than stars and planets.
- **Galaxies** are vast systems of stars, planets, and nebulae held together by gravity. Planetary systems, consisting of planets orbiting stars, are positioned within larger galaxies such as the Milky Way, which is where our planetary system, the solar system, resides. Many galaxies have a spiral shape, but there are other shapes, such as elliptical and irregular.

Stars

Constellations are small groups of stars that look like pictures in the sky. As the Earth orbits the Sun, constellations appear to be moving across the sky. However, it is the view from Earth that changes, and because of this, different stars and constellations can be seen in different seasons. For example, the constellation Pisces can be seen in late fall, and Scorpius can be seen in the summer.

Sizes of Stars

Stars come in a large variety of sizes. They can be the size of a large town or larger than the Sun. The largest stars are called **supergiant** stars, and can be 1,500 times larger than the Sun. The smallest stars are called **red dwarf** stars. The Sun is considered a medium-sized star. The size of a star can be affected by the gravitational pull acting on the star and the star's radiation. As energy is released from the center of the star, the star will grow. However, gravity from the center of the star pulls against that growth and can shrink or limit the star's size. The mass and density of the star will also generally influence its size. From Earth, scientists can determine the size of a star by the star's **luminosity**, which is the total energy a star can radiate in one second, and its **temperature**. The **Hertzsprung-Russell Diagram** was created to compare stars based on these characteristics. Stars with higher temperature and luminosity are larger in size, while stars with lower temperature and lower luminosity are smaller in size.

Brightness of Stars

The brightness of a star when viewed from Earth is its **apparent brightness**. The difference in apparent brightness among stars can be affected by two factors: the distance from the star to Earth and the amount of light put out by the star. Two stars can put out the same amount of light, but from Earth, one may appear to be dimmer than the other. That is because the one that looks dimmer is further away from Earth. The closest star to the Earth is the Sun, which is why it appears to be the brightest of all the stars from Earth. Some stars are so far away that they cannot be seen from Earth, and they may only be discovered and identified by studying the motion of other stars or planets around them. The brightness of a star will vary throughout its life cycle. The more energy a star produces, the more light it will give off. Sometimes the energy produced by a star becomes greater than the gravitational pull on the star. This causes the star to explode and create a supernova, which will shine very brightly for many days.

Characteristics of the Sun, the Moon, and Earth

The Sun, Earth, and Moon are all part of the solar system. They are all spherical in shape and rotate on their own axes. However, they each have different physical characteristics and patterns.

- **The Sun:** The Sun is much larger than Earth and is the center of the solar system. The planets orbit around it. It is made up of gases. The most abundant gas is hydrogen, but it also contains helium and a small amount of metal. The temperature of the Sun's surface is nearly 10,000 degrees Fahrenheit.
- **Earth:** Earth orbits around the Sun over the course of a year, rotating on its own axis at a constant tilt. The tilt causes the change in seasons. Earth makes one complete rotation on its axis in 24 hours. The distance between the Sun and Earth allows Earth to have a temperature that sustains life, unlike planets that are closer to, or farther away from, the Sun. Earth is made up of solids, liquids, and gases. Oxygen and iron make up the majority of Earth's mass.
- **The Moon:** The Moon also rotates on its own axis, but it orbits around Earth and is much smaller than Earth. The Moon is made up of solid rock. The surface of the Moon contains many depressions called craters.

SUN

The **Sun** is the vital force of life on Earth; it is also the central component of our solar system. It is a spherical star composed of extremely hot gases (close to 15 million degrees at the core) that are held together by gravity. Some of these gaseous molecules are ionized due to the high temperatures. The balance between its gravitational force and the pressure produced by the hot gases is called **hydrostatic equilibrium**. The source of the solar energy that keeps the Sun alive and plays a key role in the perpetuation of life on Earth is located in the Sun's core, where nucleosynthesis produces heat energy and photons. The Sun's atmosphere consists of the photosphere, the surface visible from Earth, the chromosphere, a layer outside of and hotter than the photosphere, the transition zone (the region where temperatures rise between the chromosphere and the corona), and the corona, which is best viewed at x-ray wavelengths. A solar flare is an explosive emission of ionized particles from the Sun's surface.

Review Video: The Sun
Visit mometrix.com/academy and enter code: 699233

Solar System

The *solar system* consists of the Sun and eight *major planets*. In order from the Sun the planets are Mercury, Venus, Earth, Mars, Jupiter, Saturn, Uranus and Neptune. Pluto is no longer considered to be a major planet. Along with 5 other similar sized objects it is now a *dwarf planet*. Six of the major planets have one or more moons. The solar system also contains countless *meteoroids*, *asteroids*, and *comets*.

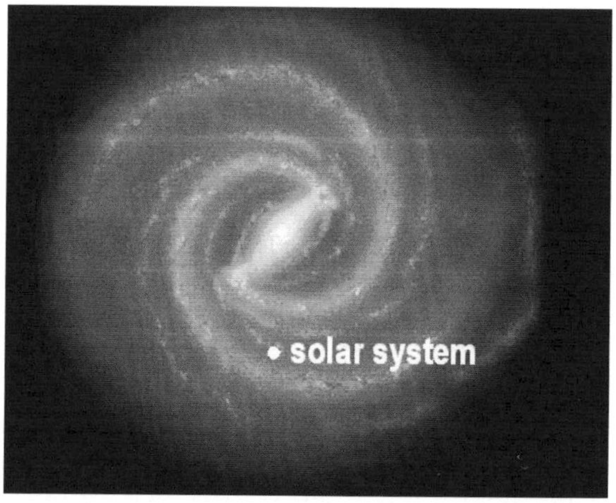

Planets

All the planets revolve around the Sun, which is an average-sized star in the spiral Milky Way galaxy. They revolve in the same direction in nearly circular orbits. If the planets were viewed by looking down from the Sun, they would rotate in a counter-clockwise direction. All the planets are in, or near, the same plane, called the ecliptic, and their axis of rotation is nearly perpendicular to the ecliptic. The only exception is Uranus, which is tipped on its side.

Terrestrial Planets, Jovian Planets, and Mass of Planets

The **Terrestrial Planets** are: Mercury, Venus, Earth, and Mars. These are the four planets closest to the Sun. They are called terrestrial because they all have a compact, rocky surface similar to the Earth's. Venus, Earth, and Mars have significant atmospheres, but Mercury has almost no atmosphere.

The **Jovian Planets** are: Jupiter (the largest planet), Saturn, Uranus, and Neptune. They are called Jovian (Jupiter-like) because of their huge sizes in relation to that of the Earth, and because they all have a gaseous nature like Jupiter. Although gas giants, some or all of the Jovian Planets may have small, solid cores.

The Sun represents 99.85% of all the matter in our solar system. Combined, the planets make up only 0.135% of the mass of the solar system, with Jupiter having twice the mass of all the other planets combined. The remaining 0.015% of the mass comes from comets, planetary satellites, asteroids, meteoroids, and interplanetary medium.

Review Video: Terrestrial Planets
Visit mometrix.com/academy and enter code: 100346

Definition of Planet

On August 24, 2006, the International Astronomical Union redefined the criteria a body must meet to be classified as a planet, stating that the following conditions must be met:

- "A planet orbits around a star and is neither a star nor a moon."
- "Its shape is spherical due to its gravity."
- "It has 'cleared' the space of its orbit."

A **dwarf planet** such as Pluto does not meet the third condition. Small solar system bodies such as asteroids and comets meet only the first condition.

Comets, Asteroids, and Meteoroids

Comets are celestial bodies composed of dust, rock, frozen gases, and ice. They range from tens of yards to tens of miles in diameter. They orbit the Sun with periods of a few years to hundreds of thousands of years. Invisible until they near the Sun, comets emit volatile components in jets of gas and dust when exposed to the Sun's heat. The **coma** is the comet's fog-like envelope that glows as it reflects sunlight and releases radiation. **Solar winds** blow a comet away from the Sun and give it a tail of dust or electrically charged molecules. Each orbit of a comet causes it to lose matter until it breaks up or vaporizes into the Sun. Halley's comet, shown below, orbits the Sun every 75 to 76 years.

Asteroids are irregularly-shaped boulders, usually less than 60 miles in diameter, that orbit the Sun. Most are made of graphite; about 25% are silicates, or iron and nickel. Collisions or gravitational forces can cause them to fly off and possibly hit a planet.

Meteoroids are fragments of asteroids of various sizes. They hurl through the solar system at speeds of between 15 and 45 miles per second. If they come through Earth's atmosphere, they are called meteors or shooting stars. In the atmosphere, they burn up and leave a visible fiery trail of gas and debris called a *meteor*. If they are large enough and do not completely burn up, they land on Earth, and they are called *meteorites*, and create craters on impact (the Barringer Crater in Arizona).

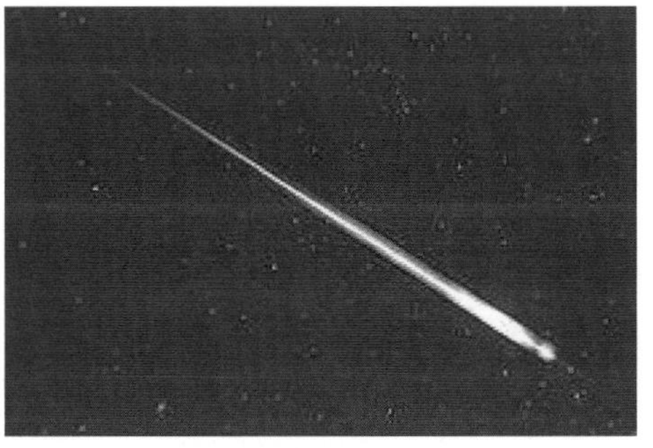

Milky Way

On a clear dark moonless night far from city lights a broad white band of stars that stretches across the sky can be seen. This is the Milky Way galaxy, and our Sun and the solar system are part of it. The Milky Way is a huge flat disk containing between 200 billion and 400 billion stars. Because Earth is in that disk, we see it edge on, which is why it appears to us as a broad band of light.

The Milky Way is a flat, disk-shaped spiral galaxy with a central bar-like bulge of stars. It is huge—between 100,000 and 120,000 light-years in diameter. A light-year is a unit of distance, not time. It is the distance light travels in one year, about 6 trillion miles. The Milky Way is between 600 thousand trillion and 700 thousand trillion miles across. Our solar system lies about two thirds of the way out on one of the spiral arms.

Earth's Revolution Around the Sun

Like all celestial objects in our solar system, **Earth** revolves around the **Sun**. This process takes approximately 365 1/4 days. This period of time is equal to a **calendar year**. The path of the orbit of Earth around the Sun is not circular, but it is **elliptical**, or shaped like an oval. Therefore, the distance between the Earth and the Sun at points on either extreme of this counterclockwise orbit are not equal. In other words, the distance between Earth and the Sun varies over the course of a year. At **perihelion**, the Earth's minimum distance from the Sun, Earth is 147 million kilometers from the Sun. At **aphelion**, the Earth's maximum distance from the Sun, Earth is 152 million kilometers from the Sun. This movement of the Earth is responsible for the apparent annual motions of the Sun (in a path referred to as the ecliptic) and other celestial objects visible from Earth's surface.

The Appearance of the Sun

The Sun is the largest object in the solar system, and it is about 109 times larger than Earth. The Earth is constantly in **orbit** around the Sun. While the Earth is in orbit, it is also **rotating** on its own **axis**. Because the Earth is always moving in this way, it appears that the Sun is moving across the sky and changing location over the course of the day. However, the Sun is not actually moving across the sky. The region of the Earth that is facing the Sun experiences daytime, while the rest of the Earth experiences nighttime. In addition, the path that the Earth travels as it orbits the Sun is not a perfect circle. It is more **elongated**, like an oval. This means that the distance from the Sun to Earth varies throughout the year. The changing distance affects how bright the Sun looks from Earth.

Earth's Rotation

The **Earth rotates** west to east about its axis, an imaginary straight line that runs nearly vertically through the center of the planet. This rotation (which takes 23 hours, 56 minutes, and 5 seconds) places each section of the Earth's surface in a position facing the Sun for a period of time. This creates the alternating periods of light and darkness we experience as **day and night**. This rotation constitutes a **sidereal day**. It is measured as the amount of time required for a reference star to cross the **meridian**, an imaginary north-south line above an observer. Each star crosses the meridian once every **sidereal** day. Since the speed at which Earth rotates is not exactly constant, we use the average **solar day** (a 24-hour period) in timekeeping rather than the slightly variable sidereal day.

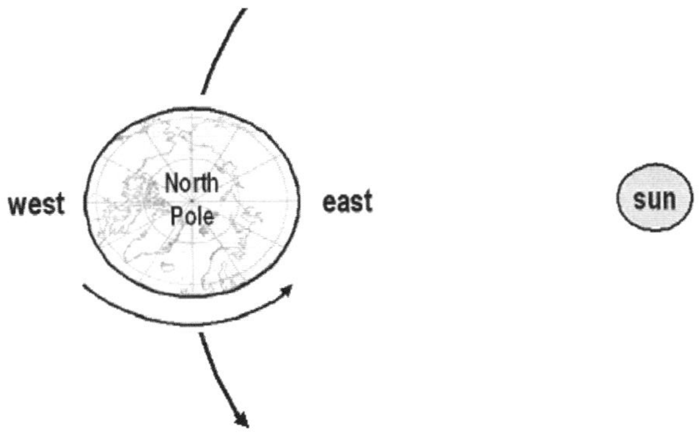

Phases of the Moon

The light of the Moon is a reflection of sunlight that reaches the Moon. The Moon is always orbiting Earth, and as Earth and the Moon both move throughout their orbits, sunlight reaches different areas of the Moon. A **moon phase** describes the appearance of the Moon. Moon phases depend on the position of the Moon, Earth, and Sun. A **new moon** occurs when the Moon is between the Sun and Earth. During this phase, the Moon is not visible because the Sun is illuminating the side of the Moon that is facing away from Earth. When any sunlight reaches the side of the Moon that is facing Earth, the appearance of the Moon will depend on its phase. For example, following a new moon, the right edge of the visible side of the Moon will look like a crescent. This phase is called a **waxing crescent**. During the next phase, the **first quarter**, the right half of the visible side of the moon will be lit up in a half-circle shape. Following that phase, the moon will then appear to be in an oval shape during its **waxing gibbous** phase. After that phase is the **full moon**, where the moon appears as a bright, white circle. Then, the Moon returns to a new moon as it goes through these phases in the opposite order and direction. These phases are known as the **waning gibbous**, **third quarter**, and **waning crescent** phases.

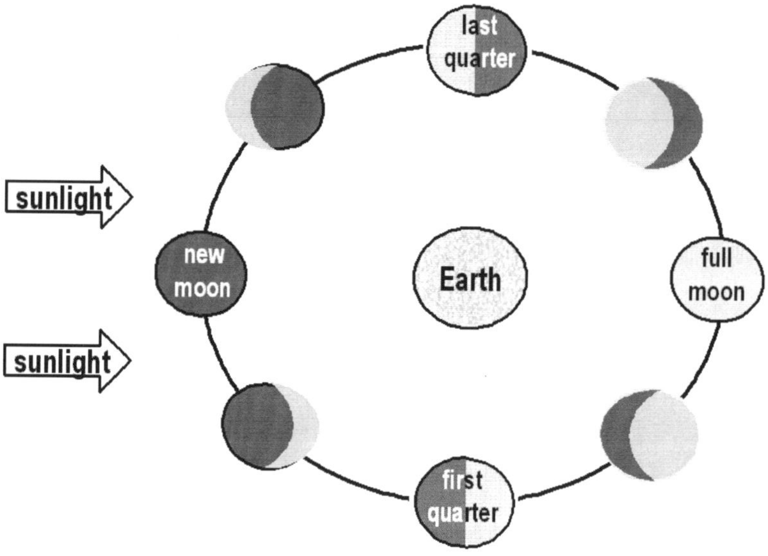

Newton's Law of Gravitation

Newton's law of gravitation (sometimes referred to as the law of universal gravitation) states that the force of gravity operates as an attractive force between all bodies in the universe. In the case of gravitation on Earth, objects behave as if there was a single particle located at the center of the Earth with the mass of the entire Earth. Thus, regardless of an object's distance from the surface of the Earth, it can be approximated as a particle due to the effective distance from the Earth's center of mass. The difference in the gravitational pull on an object at sea level and that same object at the highest point on the Earth's surface is about a quarter of a percent.

Earth's Atmosphere

Earth's gravity is strong enough to attract the molecules of the gases in the atmosphere and keep them in a layer surrounding the planet. The gravity of smaller celestial bodies like Mercury and Earth's moon is not strong enough to do this, and their atmospheres long ago diffused out into space.

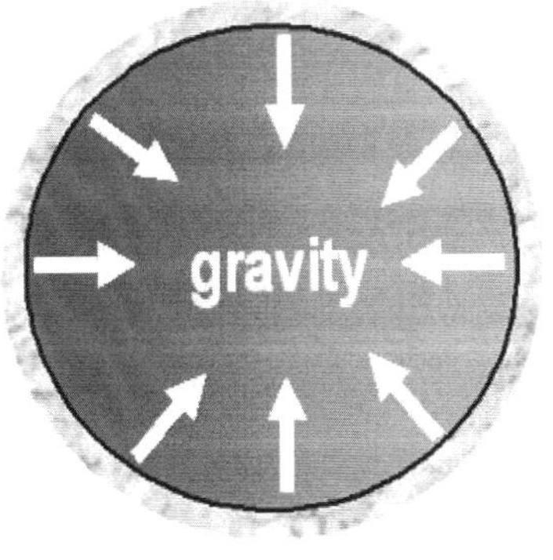

Temperature

Temperature describes the amount of **heat** in an area. The Earth's tilt and shape impact the average temperatures in each region. The Sun shines on the areas closest to the equator most directly, causing those areas to have warmer average temperatures. All other areas receive energy from the Sun at different angles, causing lower average temperatures. The farther North or South an area is from the equator, the less directly the Sun will shine on them. Since temperature is an important part of the water cycle, it also has an effect on the humidity, precipitation, and air pressure in an area. Since weather processes are like cycles, these factors can also impact the temperature in an area. Temperature can be predicted based on an area's location, the time of year, the moisture in an area, and the air pressure in an area.

Rock Cycle

The **rock cycle** is the process whereby the materials that make up the Earth transition through the three types of rock: igneous, sedimentary, and metamorphic. Rocks, like all matter, cannot be created or destroyed; rather, they undergo a series of changes and adopt different forms through the functions of the rock cycle. Plate tectonics and the water cycle are the driving forces behind the rock cycle; they force rocks and minerals out of equilibrium and force them to adjust to different external conditions. Viewed in a generalized, cyclical fashion, the rock cycle operates as follows: rocks beneath Earth's surface melt into magma. This **magma** either erupts through volcanoes or remains inside the Earth. Regardless, the magma cools, forming igneous rocks. On the surface, these rocks experience **weathering** and **erosion**, which break them down and distribute the fragments across the surface. These fragments form layers and eventually become **sedimentary rocks**. Sedimentary rocks are then either transformed to **metamorphic rocks** (which will become magma inside the Earth) or melted down into magma.

Rock Formation

Igneous Rocks: Igneous rocks can be formed from sedimentary rocks, metamorphic rocks, or other igneous rocks. Rocks that are pushed under the Earth's surface (usually due to plate subduction) are exposed to high mantle temperatures, which cause the rocks to melt into magma. The magma then rises to the surface through volcanic processes. The lower atmospheric temperature causes the magma to cool, forming grainy, extrusive igneous rocks. The creation of extrusive, or volcanic, rocks is quite rapid. The cooling process can occur so rapidly that crystals do not form; in this case, the result is a glass, such as obsidian. It is also possible for magma to cool down inside the Earth's interior; this type of igneous rock is called intrusive. Intrusive, or plutonic, rocks cool more slowly, resulting in a coarse-grained texture.

Sedimentary Rocks: Sedimentary rocks are formed when rocks at the Earth's surface experience weathering and erosion, which break them down and distribute the fragments across the surface. Fragmented material (small pieces of rock, organic debris, and the chemical products of mineral sublimation) is deposited and accumulates in layers, with top layers burying the materials beneath. The pressure exerted by the topmost layers causes the lower layers to compact, creating solid sedimentary rock in a process called lithification.

Fossil Fuels

Sedimentary rock can contain the remains of living organisms. This happens when clasts are deposited on top of remains or pieces of remains are deposited among the clasts. Over time and with pressure, these remains become substances called **fossil fuels** that can fuel machines. Some examples of fossil fuels are oil and coal.

Example

Which of the following best explains how fossil fuels are formed?

a. Fossils created from the mass extinction of dinosaurs gradually broke down into fuel such as oil.
b. Decaying plants and animals at the bottom of the ocean were compressed into fuel such as oil.
c. The remains of animals encased in ice from the last ice age melted, releasing fuel such as oil.
d. Fossils and bones are processed by humans to create fuels such as oil.

Choice A states that fossil fuels were formed from dinosaur fossils. The production of fossil fuels is unrelated to fossils, despite their name. Fossil fuels are formed from the remains of ancient plants and animals, not dinosaur fossils. Choice A is incorrect.

Choice B proposes that fossil fuels were formed from the remains of plants and animals in the ocean. Over very long periods of time, pressure and heat can turn these remains into fossil fuels. Choice B could be the correct answer.

Choice C states that fossil fuels are the result of animal remains that have become encased in ice during an ice age melting. When this happens, it typically preserves the remains of the animals, and they do not decay or transform into materials such as fossil fuels. Choice C is not the answer.

Choice D has to do with fossils being processed by humans to create fossil fuels. Fossil fuels do not actually come from fossils, and they are created through natural processes over hundreds of millions of years, not by humans. Choice D is incorrect.

Choice B is the correct answer. Fossil fuels are created not from fossils, but from decaying remains of plants and animals in the ocean due to extreme amounts of time, pressure, and heat

Metamorphic Rocks: Metamorphic rocks are igneous or sedimentary rocks that have "morphed" into another kind of rock. In metamorphism, high temperatures and levels of pressure change preexisting rocks physically and/or chemically, which produces different species of rocks. In the rock cycle, this process generally occurs in materials that have been thrust back into the Earth's mantle by plate subduction. Regional metamorphism refers to a large band of metamorphic activity; this often occurs near areas of high orogenic (mountain-building) activity. Contact metamorphism refers to metamorphism that occurs when "country rock" (that is, rock native to an area) comes into contact with high-heat igneous intrusions (magma).

Role of Water

Water plays an important role in the rock cycle through its roles in **erosion** and **weathering**: it wears down rocks; it contributes to the dissolution of rocks and minerals as acidic soil water; and it carries ions and rock fragments (sediments) to basins where they will be compressed into **sedimentary rock**. Water also plays a role in the **metamorphic processes** that occur underwater in newly-formed igneous rock at mid-ocean ridges. The presence of water (and other volatiles) is a vital component in the melting of rocky crust into magma above subduction zones.

Review Video: Igneous, Sedimentary, and Metamorphic Rocks
Visit mometrix.com/academy and enter code: 689294

Soils

Soils are formed when rock is broken down into smaller and smaller fragments by physical, chemical, and biological processes. This is called **weathering**. *Physical processes* include **erosion** and **transportation** by water and wind, freezing and thawing, and slumping due to gravity. *Chemical changes* alter the original substances present in rocks and early-stage soils. *Biological processes* include burrowing by animals like earthworms and rodents and penetration by plant roots. As plants and animals die and **decay**, soils become rich in dark organic matter called *humus*.

Properties of Soil

Since soil is a mixture of rock fragments and biological materials, it varies significantly. The composition of soil determines whether it will be good for plant life or not. Several properties of soil can be used to identify its composition, which can be helpful for adjusting it for suitability for plant growth.

- **Texture** refers to the size of the particles, which are classified as sand, silt, or clay, depending on the size and mixture of the particles.
- **Structure** refers to the density and arrangement of the soil particles. Soil can be compacted, making it dense and rock-like or it can be loose and easy to work with when planting.
- **Porosity** refers to how well water flows through the soil. A higher sand content usually allows water to flow through the soil more easily, whereas clay tends to hold onto water.

- **Chemistry** cannot be seen, but can be tested for the actual elements present in a sample of soil.
- **Color** of soil changes based on the types of minerals and organic matter in the soil. Redder soil may indicate that there is oxidized (rusted) iron in the soil, for instance.

Mineral Properties

Minerals are important because they act as the building blocks for rocks, which create the surface of the Earth. Minerals can be identified based on their many properties, which include hardness, color, luster (or shininess), cleavage (the way a mineral breaks or splits apart), and streak color (the color left after scratching a mineral against a tile). Calcite, for example, is an important mineral that is defined by its softness, white color, dullness, block-like cleavage pattern, and white streak color. Quartz, on the other hand, is defined by is hardness, varying colors, glassy luster, fracturing (breaking into pieces that are not smooth), and white streak color. While these two minerals have some similar properties, their hardness, luster, and cleavage would help scientists know they are two different minerals.

Natural Resources

The term **natural resources** refers to products and energy that can be harvested from the world and used.

- **Water** is one of the most abundant resources on the Earth and is necessary for life.
- **Natural gas** and **oil** exist underground and deep in the ocean and can be used as fuel for machines.
- **Trees** can be harvested for wood and paper and other byproducts that are used in daily life.
- **Metals** can be harvested from the ground and are used in many applications, such as building materials and in electronics.
- **Sand** can be used to make glass, soaps, and electronics.
- **Sunlight** and **wind** can be harvested with solar panels and wind turbines to generate electricity.
- **Animal products** are used for food or materials in clothing and some manufacturing processes.

Renewable and Non-renewable Resources

Materials and energy on the Earth are classified as either renewable or non-renewable. The term **renewable resources** refers to resources that are not going to run out due to overuse or can be easily reclaimed once used. This includes the sun, wind, and water. Some plants and animals grow so fast that it would be very challenging to run out and cause any form of extinction. **Non-renewable resources** include materials that take a very long time to produce, such as fossil fuels and coal. Once the Earth's population uses these materials up, it is very difficult to obtain or impossible to create more. Because renewable resources do not run out, whereas non-renewable resources do, environmentalists and scientists are always looking for new renewable resources to supply the planet with energy and for ways to reduce consumption of non-renewable resources. This reduction of consumption is known as **conservation**.

Resources Found in Florida

Many key resources are available in Florida. These include water, phosphate, oil, limestone, silicon, wind, and solar energy. Found in the ocean, rivers, and lakes of Florida, water is a crucial resource that is renewable thanks to the water cycle. Water is used as a source of power, in manufacturing goods, in growing crops, and for consumption. Wind is a renewable energy source in Florida that is harnessed using wind turbines offshore. Solar energy is another important renewable energy source that can be harnessed using solar panels. Made of several minerals containing phosphorus, phosphate is nonrenewable resource mined in Florida to make fertilizers and other products. Another important nonrenewable resource is oil, which is mined around Florida and often used to make gas for cars or other vehicles. Limestone is a nonrenewable rock that is mined and used in buildings and roads. Silicon is another nonrenewable resource mined in Florida that is used in computers and other electronics.

Water Cycle

The **water cycle** refers to the circulation of water in the Earth's hydrosphere (below the surface, on the surface, and above the surface of the Earth). This continuous process involves five physical actions.

- **Evaporation** refers to liquid water heating up and changing to into a gas, known as water vapor.
- **Transpiration** is where water inside of plants evaporates directly out of plant leaves.
- **Condensation** refers to the water vapor cooling down and beginning to turn back into a liquid form, causing clouds to form.
- **Precipitation** refers to the rain, snow, hail, or sleet that falls from clouds once the water vapor has condensed enough.
- The **storage** stage of the water cycle refers to water being stored in the ground, trees, or bodies of water on the Earth. Water is trapped in vegetation, collected in bodies of water on the Earth's surface, or absorbed into the Earth's surface. **Runoff**, caused by gravity, physically moves water downward into oceans or other water bodies.

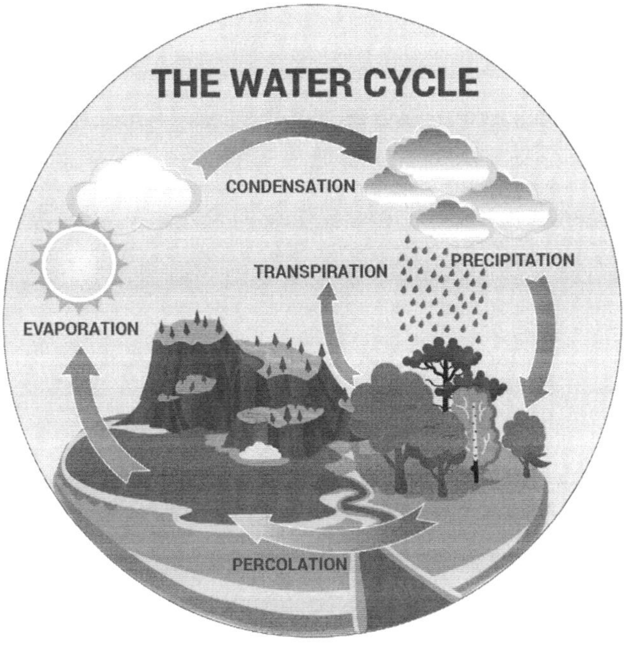

Review Video: Hydrologic Cycle
Visit mometrix.com/academy and enter code: 426578

Roles of the Sun and the Ocean in the Water Cycle

More than 96% of the Earth's water is in the oceans, and the oceans cover more than 70% of the Earth's surface. Ocean water plays a major role in the water cycle. The Sun is also extremely important to the water cycle because it heavily impacts the temperature of the water that sits on Earth's surface. As sunlight hits the surface of the ocean, water heats and begins to **evaporate**. It becomes **water vapor**, which is a gas. The water vapor rises into the atmosphere and **condenses** to form **clouds**. These clouds travel and move across the Earth due to air currents. As more water evaporates and condenses, the clouds become heavy and begin to **precipitate**. This results in **rain**, which collects on the Earth's surface and provides water for living things that need it to survive. These processes also help to regulate the Earth's temperature and prevent large changes in temperature.

Weather

Heat energy from the Sun warms different parts of the planet in different ways at different times. As warm air rises it expands and cools. This causes moisture to condense as liquid drops or freeze as ice crystals to form clouds. When the water drops or ice crystals become too large to stay aloft, they fall as precipitation. As warm air rises it also leaves a low pressure zone behind. This causes air from high surrounding high pressure zones to rush in as wind.

Clouds

Clouds form when water vapor in the atmosphere cools to the point where it condenses out as water droplets or small particles of frozen ice crystals that we can see. Clouds can also form when more moisture is added to the air by evaporation until the air becomes saturated and cannot hold any more water. Then the water vapor will begin to condense into visible droplets.

Precipitation

Precipitation is water that falls back to the surface of the Earth from the atmosphere. This water may be in the form of **rain**, which is water in liquid form. Raindrops are formed in clouds due to **condensation**. When the drops become too large to remain in the clouds, gravity causes them to fall toward the surface of the Earth. Extremely small raindrops are called **drizzle**. If the temperature of a layer of air through which rain passes is below the freezing point of water, the rain may take the form of **sleet**, which is partially frozen water. Precipitation may also fall in the form of **snow**, which is made of ice crystals. When clumps of snowflakes melt and refreeze, **hail** is formed. Hail may also be formed when liquid water gathers on the surface of a snowflake and then freezes.

Wind

When the Sun shines, it heats the surface of Earth, including Earth's atmosphere. This heating does not occur evenly because some places on Earth, such as the equator, receive more direct sunlight than others. When air is heated and becomes warmer, it rises due to decreased density, causing more dense air from colder parts of the planet to rush in under it. As the warm air moves in the atmosphere, it cools and begins to sink again. This creates a cycle of heat movement within Earth's atmosphere called **convection**. This circular motion of air in the atmosphere is responsible for winds.

Air Pressure

Pressure describes the amount of force applied to an object over a certain area. For example, a person standing on a bed sinks deeper into the bed than a person laying on it. This occurs because the same amount of force is applied to a smaller area, which means the pressure is higher. Pressure applies to all forces that are applied to other objects, including air. The pressure applied by air in a given place is called **air pressure**, or **barometric pressure**. Because air has mass, and gravity is pulling it toward the Earth, air applies force on everything beneath it. Air pressure changes with **altitude**, which is the height of an object above sea level. The lower the altitude, the higher the air pressure. This is because the air at higher altitudes is weighing on the air underneath it. Similarly, air pressure is lower at higher altitudes.

Impact of Temperature and Humidity on Air Pressure

Humidity and temperature also affect air pressure. **Humidity** refers to how much moisture is in the air. Air that contains more water molecules contains more mass than drier air. Therefore, gravity pulls more on air that has higher humidity, which causes increased air pressure. Similarly, **temperature** can affect the density of air. Gases do not have a constant volume, but the space between the molecules in a gas grows and shrinks with changes in temperature, causing changes in air pressure.

Impact of Air Pressure on Climate and Weather

Weather systems are often described based on air pressure. A **high-pressure system** means that an area has higher air pressure, while a **low-pressure system** has a lower pressure. Pressure will move toward **equilibrium**, or a state of **balance**. Therefore, high- and low-pressure systems naturally interact with each other. Low pressure systems try to **pull air** toward them to reach equilibrium. This causes condensation to form and can eventually produce storms. High pressure systems **push air** away from them and are usually associated with sunny or clear weather.

Pressure Systems

The atoms in warm air are less densely packed, causing them to exert less pressure. In contrast, cold air is characterized by closely packed atoms, which means it has high density and exerts much pressure. A **low-pressure system** attracts air from surrounding areas, causing it to rise and condense higher in the atmosphere, leading to clouds and precipitation such as rain. A **high-pressure system** blows air away from itself and is associated with fewer clouds and calmer weather. The boundary where two systems interact is called a **front** and is associated with turbulent, stormy weather. Scientists like **meteorologists** use **pressure maps** to predict the weather, usually for a specific area that is local to them. By mapping out the location of high- and low-pressure systems and examining the boundaries between them, meteorologists can predict future weather based on the weather patterns associated with each system and type of boundary.

Measuring Weather

Weather can be measured by a variety of methods. The simplest include measurement of rainfall, sunshine, pressure, humidity, temperature, and cloudiness with basic instruments such as thermometers, barometers, and rain gauges. However, the use of **radar** (which involves analysis of microwaves reflecting off of raindrops) and satellite imagery grants meteorologists a look at the big picture of weather across, for example, an entire continent. This helps them understand and make predictions about current and developing weather systems. Infrared (heat-sensing) imaging allows meteorologists to measure the temperature of clouds above ground. Using weather reports gathered from different weather stations spread over an area, meteorologists create synoptic charts. The locations and weather reports of several stations are plotted on a chart; analysis of the pressures reported from each location, as well as rainfall, cloud cover, and so on, can reveal basic weather patterns.

Climate Zones

Plains are extensive areas of low-lying, flat, or gently undulating land, and are usually lower than the landforms around them. Plains near the seacoast are called lowlands. Humidity and temperature vary in these regions depending on the location. Plain regions are also known for having strong winds.

Deserts are large, dry areas that receive less than 10 inches of rain per year. They are almost barren, containing only a few patches of vegetation. Deserts typically have very low humidity levels and very high temperatures.

Mountains are elevated landforms that rise fairly steeply from the earth's surface to a summit of at least 1,000-2,000 feet (definitions vary) above sea level. Temperatures typically are lower on mountains compared to other regions since they are elevated in Earth's atmosphere.

Marshes and swamps are both **wet lowlands**. The water can be fresh, brackish, or saline. Both host important ecological systems with unique wildlife. There are, however, some major differences. **Marshes** have no trees and are always wet because of frequent floods and poor drainage that leaves shallow water. Plants are mostly grasses, rushes, reeds, typhas, sedges, and herbs. **Swamps** have trees and dry periods. The water is very slow-moving, and is usually associated with adjacent rivers or lakes. Both of these regions typically have warmer temperatures and higher humdity levels.

Both taiga and tundra regions have many plants and animals, but they have few humans or crops because of their harsh climates. **Taiga** has colder winters and hotter summers than tundra because of its distance from the Arctic Ocean. Taiga is the world's largest forest region, located just south of the tundra line. It contains huge mineral resources and fur-bearing animals. **Tundra** is a Russian word describing marshy plain in an area that has a very cold climate but receives little snow. The ground is usually frozen, but is quite spongy when it is not. The humidity ranges in these regions, but, overall, it typically remains relatively low.

A **humid continental climate** is one that has four seasons, including a cold winter and a hot summer, and sufficient rainfall for raising crops. Such climates can be found in the United States, Canada, and Russia. The best farmlands and mining areas are found in these countries.

Prairie climates, or steppe regions, are found in the interiors of Asia and North America where there are dry flatlands (prairies that receive 10-20 inches of rain per year). These dry flatlands can be grasslands or deserts.

Subtropical climates are very humid areas in the tropical areas of Japan, China, Australia, Africa, South America, and the United States. The moisture, carried by winds traveling over warm ocean currents, produces long summers and mild winters. It is possible to produce a continuous cycle of a variety of crops.

A **marine climate** is one near or surrounded by water. Warm ocean winds bring moisture, mild temperatures year-round, and plentiful rain. These climates are found in Western Europe and parts of the United States, Canada, Chile, New Zealand, and Australia.

Review Video: Climates
Visit mometrix.com/academy and enter code: 991320

Climate Zones Related to Location and Elevation

Climate zones, such as polar, tropical, and temperate locations, are defined by their temperature and precipitation. This correlates to a location's latitude, elevation, and closeness to water. Higher latitudes like the North and South Poles are usually cold and dry. Latitudes closer to the equator are much warmer and more humid, in part because these areas receive more solar energy. Similarly, higher elevations are typically colder and less humid because precipitation freezes at greater heights. Closeness to bodies of water typically results in a more temperate climate since the water absorbs heat and cools slowly, keeping the seasons moderate but with much more precipitation than other areas. Polar zones are more likely to be at high elevations and higher latitudes with less rainfall. Tropical zones are more likely to be at lower elevations, near the equator, and around bodies of water. Temperate zones are typically at a medium latitude and elevation.

Important Terms Related to Maps

The most important terms used when describing items on a map or globe are:

- **Latitude and longitude** – Latitude and longitude are the imaginary lines (horizontal and vertical, respectively) that divide the globe into a grid. Both are measured using the 360 degrees of a circle.
- **Coordinates** – These are the latitude and longitude measures for a place.
- **Absolute location** – This is the exact spot where coordinates meet. The grid system allows the location of every place on the planet to be identified.
- **Equator** – This is the line at 0° latitude that divides the earth into two equal halves called hemispheres.
- **Parallels** – This is another name for lines of latitude because they circle the earth in parallel lines that never meet.
- **Meridians** – This is another name for lines of longitude. The Prime Meridian is located at 0° longitude, and is the starting point for measuring distance (both east and west) around the globe. Meridians circle the earth and connect at the Poles.

Review Video: Elements of a Map
Visit mometrix.com/academy and enter code: 437727

Review Video: Map Projections
Visit mometrix.com/academy and enter code: 327303

Hemispheres and Parallels on the World Map

The definitions for these terms are as follows:

- **Northern Hemisphere** – This is the area above, or north, of the equator.
- **Southern Hemisphere** – This is the area below, or south, of the equator.
- **Western Hemisphere** – This is the area between the North and South Poles. It extends west from the Prime Meridian to the International Date Line.
- **Eastern Hemisphere** – This is the area between the North and South Poles. It extends east from the Prime Meridian to the International Date Line.
- **North and South Poles** – Latitude is measured in terms of the number of degrees north and south from the equator. The North Pole is located at 90°N latitude, while the South Pole is located at 90°S latitude.
- **Tropic of Cancer** – This is the parallel, or latitude, 23½° north of the equator.
- **Tropic of Capricorn** – This is the parallel, or latitude, 23½° south of the equator. The region between these two parallels is the tropics. The subtropics is the area located between 23½° and 40° north and south of the equator.
- **Arctic Circle** – This is the parallel, or latitude, 66½° north of the equator.
- **Antarctic Circle** – This is the parallel, or latitude, 66½° south of the equator.

Review Video: Geographical Features
Visit mometrix.com/academy and enter code: 773539

Chapter Quiz

1. Students are playing a guessing game in science class. The clue the teacher read is shown below.

> I am a star. Many objects including planets and asteroids revolve around me. What am I?

a. Sun
b. Moon
c. Comet
d. Black hole

2. Raul and Rebecca were both given a bag of ice. Raul placed his bag of ice under a shade tree, and Rebecca placed her bag of ice in the middle of the track. It was very sunny that day, and when the students returned an hour later, Raul's bag still contained several ice cubes, while Rebecca's bag was now completely water. Why did this happen?

a. The bag of ice heated more quickly in the sun than in the shady area.
b. Students probably stepped on the bag of ice that was on the track.
c. The bag of ice was protected on the track, but not under the shade tree.
d. The bag of ice heated more quickly in the shady area.

3. Antonio went outside last Monday and noticed a full moon in the sky. About how long will it take for Antonio to see the next completely full moon?

a. 30 days or one month
b. 7 days or one week
c. 60 days or 2 months
d. 365 days or 1 year

4. Angelica wrote an essay about stars, but she made one mistake. What was her mistake?

Stars

> A star is a celestial body that is made up of gas. There are many, many stars in the galaxy. Stars are different sizes. Stars can also have a different level of brightness. Stars that are closer to Earth seem less bright. The Sun is a star.

a. There are many stars in the galaxy.
b. Stars are different sizes.
c. Stars have different levels of brightness.
d. Stars closer to Earth seem less bright.

5. Earth rotates on its axis every 24 hours and revolves around the Sun every 365 earth days. Mars revolves around the Sun every 687 earth days. What does a period 687 earth days represent in terms of Mars time?

a. One Martian day
b. One Martian year
c. One Martian season
d. One Martian month

6. Which statement is true about these bolded areas near the equator.

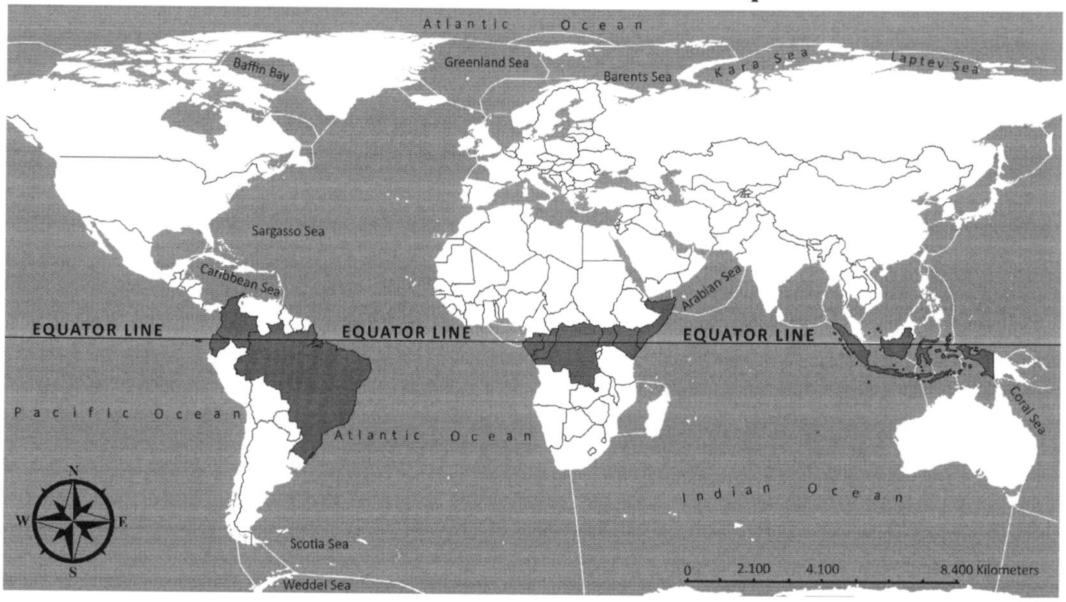

a. These areas receive a high average snowfall each year.
b. These areas are completely surrounded by water.
c. These areas usually have a very warm climate.
d. These areas have a lower temperature when compared to other areas.

7. A diagram of the water cycle is shown below. An important step of the water cycle is labeled with an "X."

What is the main source for this step of the water cycle?

a. Lakes and rivers
b. Melted glaciers
c. Oceans
d. Ponds and lakes

8. A scientist in Florida charted the celestial objects in the sky on the first day of summer and then again on the first day of winter. The scientist noticed that different stars were present in the sky during the summer than in the winter. Which statement below explains why different stars can be seen in the summer and the winter?

a. The Earth rotates on its axis once about every 24 hours.
b. The Earth orbits the Sun once a year.
c. The moon orbits the Earth in an elliptical shape.
d. The stars move in a circular orbit around the Earth

9. As a part of a project about the weather differences in various environments, Ashley made the chart below to show the averages for two areas.

	Area 1	Area 2
Temperature	105°F	30°F
Precipitation	0 cm	3 cm snow
Humidity	1%	50%
Wind	0 mph from the South	20 mph from the North

Which could be the areas described in Ashley's chart?

a. Area 1: tropical rainforest, Area 2: Saharan desert
b. Area 1: mountain peak, Area 2: Saharan desert
c. Area 1: tropical rainforest, Area 2: Artic tundra
d. Area 1: Saharan desert, Area 2: mountain peak

10. The Tibesti Mountains are in the Sahara Desert. The Arctic Cordillera Mountain Range is in the arctic tundra. Which statement below correctly describes the desert mountain temperatures compared to the arctic tundra mountain temperatures?

a. The temperatures in mountains located in the Arctic tundra would generally be much higher than the temperatures in the mountains located in the Sahara Desert.
b. The temperatures in the mountains located in the Sahara Desert would generally be much higher than the temperatures in the mountains located in the Arctic tundra.
c. The temperatures in the mountains located in the Arctic tundra would generally be about the same as the temperatures in the mountains located in the Sahara Desert.
d. The temperatures in the mountains located in the Sahara Desert would generally be lower than the Arctic tundra in the winter but higher in the summer.

Chapter Quiz Answers and Explanations

1. A: The clue is describing the Sun because the Sun is a star that planets and asteroids revolve around. Moons revolve around planets. Comets are frozen gases and rocks that revolve around the sun. Black holes are empty places in outer space where the pull of gravity is very strong.

2. A: The bag of ice melted on the track because it received radiant energy from the Sun and was heated more quickly than the bag of ice that was in the shade and therefore not receiving direct radiant energy. Human interaction was not the cause of the ice melting and not melting. The bag of ice was not protected on the track. The ice heated more quickly on the track, not in the shady area.

3. A: It takes approximately 30 days, or one month, for the moon to complete all its phases. In one week, the moon would only have moved from a full moon to almost half-moon. In two months, the moon would have been a full moon twice. In a year the moon will have gone through each phase about 12 times.

4. D: Stars that are closer to Earth seem brighter than stars that are further away. The Sun seems so bright because it is the closest star to Earth. It is true that all galaxies are made up of many, many stars, and stars have different sizes and brightness.

5. B: A year is determined by the number of days it takes for a body to make one revolution around the Sun, so a Martian year would be the number of days it takes for Mars to orbit the Sun.

6. C: Areas near the equator have a tropical climate with very warm temperatures. The warmer temperatures do not allow for a high average of snowfall. Although some areas border the ocean, not all the areas are surrounded by water. These areas would have a higher average temperature since they are so close to the equator.

7. C: The "X" indicates the process of evaporation on the water cycle diagram. The main water source for evaporation is the oceans as the oceans make up most of the water sources on our planet. Lakes, rivers, melted glaciers, and ponds contain water, but not nearly as much water as the oceans.

8. B: Different stars can be seen during different seasons because of the location of the Earth in its orbit around the Sun. The Earth's rotation on its axis is responsible for night and day. The moon orbiting the Earth explains the different moon phases. Stars do not orbit the Earth, they appear to move because of the Earth's orbit around the Sun.

9. D: Area 1 is very hot with little rainfall. This type of weather is consistent with a desert environment, such as the Saharan desert. Area 2 is cold with snow. This type of weather is consistent with a mountain peak because of its higher altitude. A tropical rainforest would receive rain, and Area 1 did not. The temperatures in Area 2 are too cold for a Saharan desert. Area 1 is too warm for a mountain peak or Arctic tundra. Snow would not be expected in a tropical rainforest.

10. B: Deserts, such as the Sahara, are known for their hot temperatures and dry conditions. A tundra, such as the ones found in the Arctic, are known for very cold temperatures and snowy conditions. The temperatures of the mountains in the desert would be expected to be much higher than the temperatures of the mountains in the Arctic tundra. The temperatures would not be the same because the climate of a desert is very different from the climate of a tundra. Winters in the desert have higher temperatures than winters in the Arctic tundra.

Physical Science

Properties of Matter

Matter is anything that takes up space and has weight. Even air has weight and takes up space. All types of matter have different properties that can be observed or measured. There are many properties of matter, including temperature, mass, magnetism, and the ability to sink or float.

Intensive and Extensive Physical Properties of Matter

Intensive properties are properties that do not change when the size of a material changes. Density, melting point, freezing point, boiling point, color, chemical reactivity, luster, malleability, and electrical conductivity are examples of intensive properties. In contrast, **extensive properties** do change when the size of a material changes. Volume, mass, and weight are examples of extensive properties. Some intensive properties can be known just by looking at an object, such as color and state of matter. Other intensive and extensive properties can only be measured using special tools or by using tests to learn more about an object. Properties that must be measured or found using tests include density, mass, volume, solubility, magnetism, and conductivity.

Temperature

Temperature is a property that tells how hot or cold a thing is. **Temperature** also demonstrates how much **thermal energy** is in a thing. When an object is cold, it has very little thermal energy. For many substances, being hot makes the substance expand, while being cold makes it shrink. Temperature also tends to transfer from one object to another. For instance, when a cup is filled with ice and water, the ice and water exchange energy until they are the same temperature. The ice and water reach the same temperature eventually, usually resulting in the ice melting.

Mass and Weight

Mass is a measure of how much **matter** is in an object. **Mass** is usually measured by placing an object on a scale. The terms mass and weight are often used interchangeably, but they actually have different definitions. Mass is always the same for a specific object, but **weight** depends on other factors. For instance, 1,000 lb. car always has the same mass, but it would weigh different amounts depending on if the car were on Earth or on Mars, which has much lower gravity.

Volume and Density

Volume is a measure of the **size** of an object or how much space an object takes up. Volume affects several other factors like density. Density is the amount of **mass** (amount of matter) in a certain **volume**. The more matter there is, the more mass an object has. **Density** takes into account both the mass and volume of an object. For instance, an inflated balloon has very little mass in it, but it is fairly large. A watermelon is about the same size, but has much more mass in it, so the watermelon is denser than the balloon. Density is the reason things float or sink. One example is oil and water. Oil is usually thicker than water, but it is actually less dense. If you put oil and water in a cup, you can see that the oil always **floats** to the top. Another way of thinking about it is that the water is actually **sinking** in the oil.

DENSITY OF WATER

Density is the **mass** (amount of matter) in a certain **volume**. The more **matter** there is, the more the object weighs. Most solids have more matter than the same volume of their liquids. This means that they are denser and sink in their own liquid. However, water is different. The molecules in ice are farther apart than they are in liquid water. That means that ice has less matter in it than the same volume of liquid water. Therefore, ice is less dense and floats in water.

MATERIALS DENSER THAN WATER

Ships and other floating objects made of materials that are denser than water float because of the empty space they contain inside their hulls. A ship weighing 5,000 tons overall will displace 5,000 tons of water, but this weight of water will occupy a smaller volume than the ship itself. Once this amount of water has been displaced the ship will not sink any deeper into the water and will float. Archimedes' principle states that the buoyant force is equal to the weight of the water (or any other fluid displaced). The reason a solid piece of iron or a rock sinks is that it weighs more than the volume of water it displaces. For the same reason, because a helium-filled balloon is lighter than air it will rise until the air's density is reduced such that the volume of air displaced is the same as the volume of the balloon.

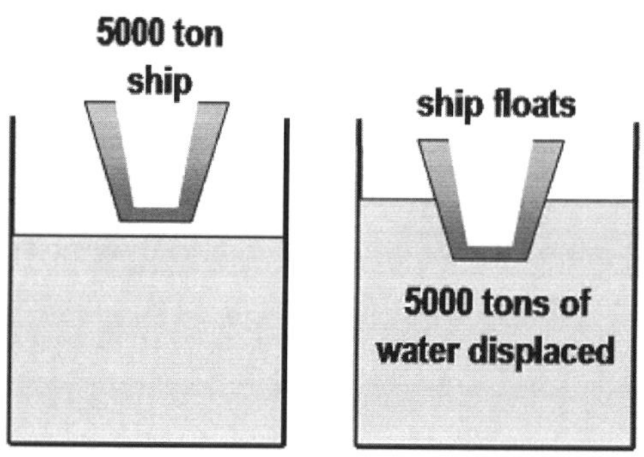

DENSITY OF WATER AND ICE

Most solids have more matter than the same volume of their liquids. This means that they are denser and sink in their own liquid. However, water is different. The molecules in ice are farther apart than they are in liquid water. That means that ice has less matter in it than the same volume of liquid water. Therefore, ice is less dense and floats in water.

MAGNETISM

Magnetism is a property that some rocks or metals can possess. **Magnetism** is a force that can push or pull on other magnetic materials. Magnets always have two poles, which attract the opposite pole and repel the same pole. Usually, the poles on a magnet are identified as being North or South, because the Earth's North and South Poles are actually magnetic as well. This is the reason that compasses work. The small needle in a compass is attracted to the Earth's poles and points in that direction. Many types of technology use magnetism, including electronics, motors, credit cards, and others.

MAGNETS

A **magnet** is any object or material, such as iron, steel, or magnetite (lodestone), that can affect another substance within its **field of force** that has like characteristics. A magnetic field is mapped by invisible curved lines of force that attract magnets or certain metals like iron or nickel. A simple bar magnet has a south pole (S) at one end and a north pole (N) at the other. Each pole will attract the opposite pole of another magnet and repel the same pole. The north pole of a compass needle will point to the south pole of a magnet, while the south pole of the needle will be attracted to the north pole of the magnet.

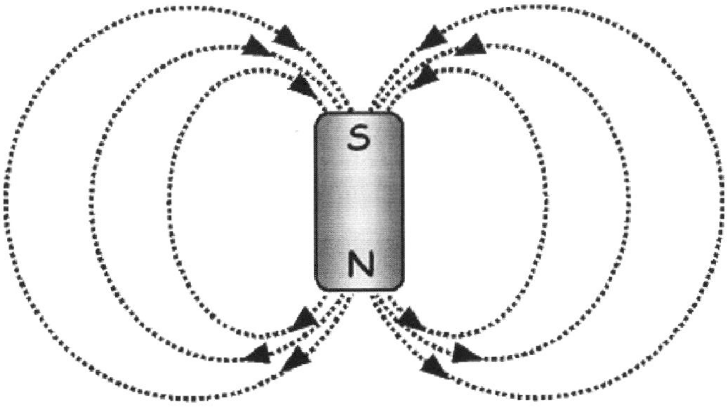

Opposite Poles of Two Magnets Attract Each Other

When two bar magnets are lined end to end with the north and south poles near each other, the lines of force run from the north pole of one magnet to the south pole of the other magnet indicating attraction.

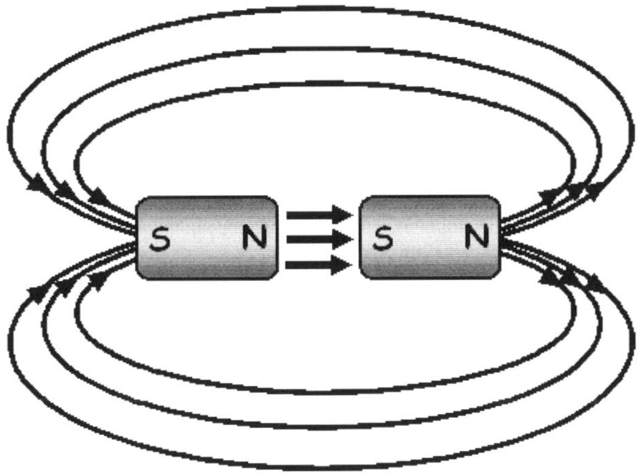

Cutting a Bar Magnet in Two

If a bar magnet is cut in two, two complete magnets will form, each with a north and south pole. If a bar magnet is cut it into three parts, three magnets will form.

POLES OF TWO MAGNETS REPEL EACH OTHER

When the like poles of two magnets are brought close to each other the lines of force run in opposite directions. This causes the two poles to push each other away.

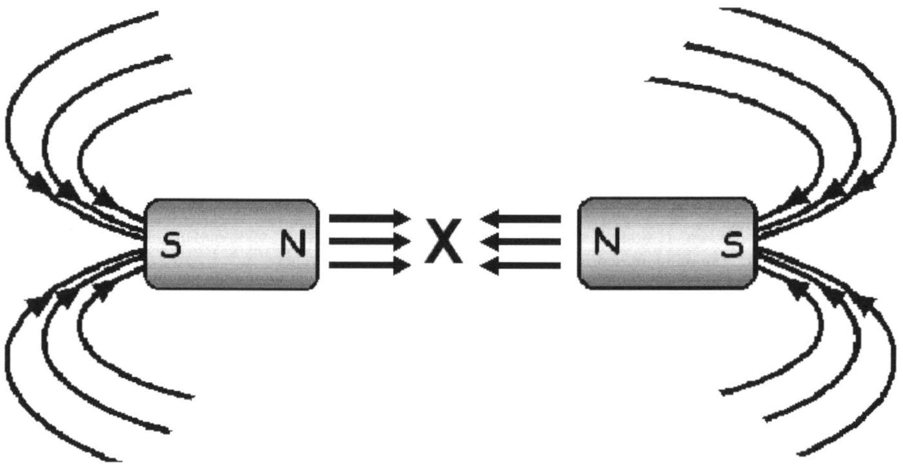

NEEDLE OF A MAGNETIC COMPASS

Planet Earth has a magnetic field just like a bar magnet. The north pole of a compass needle points to Earth's north pole because the magnetic pole near the North Pole is actually the south pole of Earth's magnetic field. Likewise, the south pole of the compass needle is attracted to the north pole of Earth's magnetic field near the south geographic pole. Just remember that each magnetic pole is attracted to its opposite pole on another magnet or magnetic object.

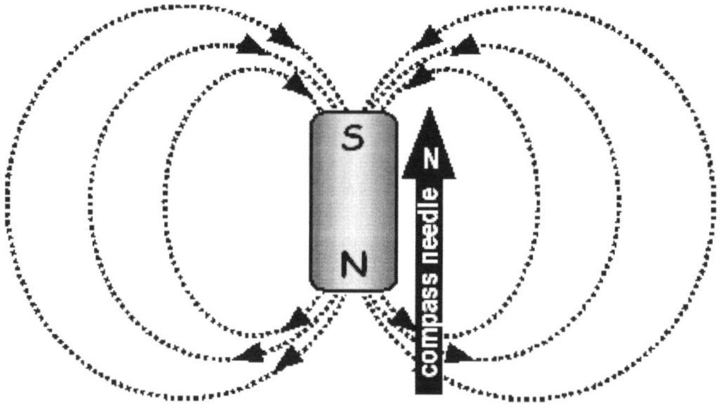

CONDUCTIVITY

Conductivity is a property that describes how easily a material **transfers energy** to and from other materials. **Conductivity** usually refers to either heat energy or electrical energy. For instance, metals are usually good at conducting both heat and electricity, whereas plastic usually is not good at conducting these types of energy. Materials that are good at transferring energy are known as **conductors**, whereas materials that are not good at transferring energy are known as **resistors**.

Physical and Chemical Changes

PHYSICAL CHANGES

Physical changes are those that do not affect the chemical properties of a substance. Changes in state are **physical changes**. For example, a liquid can freeze into a solid or boil into a gas without changing the chemical nature of the substance. It is all still the same substance. Ice, steam, and liquid water are all still water, H_2O. Physical properties include such features as shape, texture, size, volume, mass, and density. Cutting, melting, dissolving, mixing, breaking, and crushing are all types of physical changes.

CHEMICAL CHANGES

Chemical changes occur when chemical bonds are broken and new ones are formed. The original substances are **transformed** into different substances. If vinegar and baking soda are mixed together, a lot of bubbles (carbon dioxide) and water will form. Burning wood in a fireplace is another type of chemical change. The carbon in the wood reacts with oxygen in the air to make ash, carbon dioxide, smoke and energy that we feel as heat and see as light. When iron rusts, iron oxide is formed, indicating a chemical change. Other examples of chemical changes include baking a cake, digesting food, and mixing an acid and a base.

Examples of chemical changes include the following:

- (a) The temperature of a system changes without any heating or cooling.
- (b) The formation of a gas (bubbles).
- (c) The formation of a precipitate (solid) when two liquids are mixed.
- (d) A liquid changes color.

A **chemical change** occurs when two or more substances come together and interact in such a way that they become completely new substances. For example, two hydrogen atoms and one oxygen atom combine to make a new compound—a water molecule, H_2O. Likewise, two oxygen atoms and one carbon atom combine to make one molecule of carbon dioxide—CO_2. The two substances that combine are called **reactants,** and the new compound that emerges is the **product**. Chemical reactions (changes) can be much more complicated than this.

States of Matter

The three states of matter are solid, liquid, and gas. A **solid** has an exact shape and an exact volume. In a **solid**, the molecules are close together and locked into place. A **liquid** has an exact volume but does not have an exact shape. Because the molecules in a liquid move freely, liquids take the shape of their containers. Molecules in liquid have more space between them than molecules in solids do, but they do not move farther away from each other. A **gas** has no exact shape or volume. Gas particles are also free to move, and they move far away from each other so they can fill their containers. Gas particles usually have large spaces between them.

Solid	Liquid	Gas
Have a definite shape and size. Usually denser than liquids and gases of the same material.	Have a definite size, but do not have a definite shape.	Does not have a definite size or shape, but matches its container.
• Rocks • Ice Cream • Pencils • Apples	• Milk • Water • Juice • Rain	• Steam • Fire • Helium • Fog

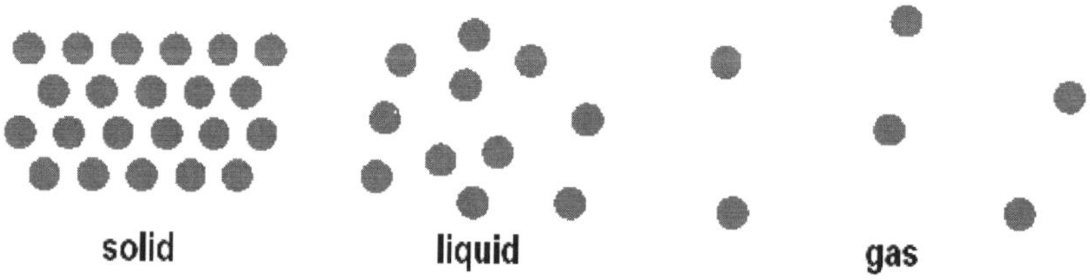

Review Video: States of Matter
Visit mometrix.com/academy and enter code: 742449

The following table shows similarities and differences between solids, liquids, and gases:

	Solid	Liquid	Gas
Shape	Fixed shape	No fixed shape (assumes shape of container)	No fixed shape (assumes shape of container)
Volume	Fixed	Fixed	Changes to assume shape of container
Fluidity	Does not flow easily	Flows easily	Flows easily
Compressibility	Hard to compress	Hard to compress	Compresses

Phase States of Water

Water has three states of matter: ice, liquid water, and water vapor. Water freezes at 32 degrees Fahrenheit, where ice crystals form and the substance becomes a solid.

- **Ice** - Water crystalizes when it freezes, which means that it actually expands when it freezes, making it less dense than liquid water. This is uncommon because solids are usually the most dense form of a substance because the atoms are more tightly compressed. That is why ice actually floats in liquid water, rather than sinks.

- **Water Vapor** – Water exists in gas form as it evaporates or boils. Water vapor exists in the air and is often referred to as humidity. There is always some moisture in the air, though as the temperatures drop or pressure changes, it will condense and become liquid water again. Just like all other gas forms, water vapor spreads out in its container and flows much like a liquid.
- **Liquid Water** – Liquid water is the most common form on Earth. Water is needed for life and makes up most of the matter in a human body. Liquid water follows all of the typical rules for liquids, including taking the shape of its container, but has a constant mass and volume.

Six Different Types of Phase Change

A substance that is undergoing a change from a solid to a liquid is said to be melting. If this change occurs in the opposite direction, from liquid to solid, this change is called freezing. A liquid which is being converted to a gas is undergoing vaporization. The reverse of this process is known as condensation. Direct transitions from gas to solid and solid to gas are much less common in everyday life, but they can occur given the proper conditions. Solid to gas conversion is known as sublimation, while the reverse is called deposition.

Review Video: Chemical and Physical Properties of Matter
Visit mometrix.com/academy and enter code: 717349

Review Video: States of Matter [Advanced]
Visit mometrix.com/academy and enter code: 298130

Mixture, Solution, and Colloid

A **mixture** is made of two or more substances that are combined in various proportions. The exact proportion of the constituents is the defining characteristic of any mixture. There are two types of mixtures: homogeneous and heterogeneous. **Homogeneous** means that the mixture's composition and properties are uniform throughout. Conversely, **heterogeneous** means that the mixture's composition and properties are not uniform throughout.

Solutions and Solubility

A **solution** is a homogeneous mixture of substances that cannot be separated by filtration or centrifugation. Solutions are made by dissolving one or more solutes into a solvent. For example, in a solution of sugar and water, sugar is the solute and water is the solvent. If there is more than one liquid present in the solution, then the most prevalent liquid is considered the solvent. The exact mechanism of dissolving varies depending on the mixture, but the result is always individual solute ions or molecules surrounded by solvent molecules. The proportion of solute to solvent for a particular solution is its **concentration**. Not all materials are able to be dissolved. Sugar is considered **soluble** in water, but sand does not dissolve in water, so it is considered **insoluble** in water.

A **colloid** is a heterogeneous mixture in which small particles (<1 micrometer) are suspended, but not dissolved, in a liquid. As such, they can be separated by centrifugation. A commonplace example of a colloid is milk.

Physical Properties of Mixtures and Solutions

When making a mixture or solution of ingredients, a person is not making a chemical change to the ingredients. Since the original ingredients are still present, their **physical properties** are usually still observable in the final mixture. Take, for instance, a solution of salt and water. The salt dissolves completely in the water, but since the salt is still present, the solution then tastes salty. Other properties, such as magnetism, do not transfer to the whole mixture. If a person were to mix sand and iron filings, then wave a magnet over the mixture, the iron filings would separate out, leaving only sand behind.

Types of Energy

Performing work or moving an object is a function of **energy**. The **law of conservation of energy** states that energy cannot be created or destroyed. Energy can only be changed to another form. Therefore, energy is always part of a pattern, cycle, or system. Two common forms of energy are potential energy and kinetic energy. **Potential energy** is energy that is **stored** in matter. If an object or organism moves or is moved, its potential energy will become kinetic energy. **Kinetic energy** is the energy of **motion**. Therefore, energy used during movement is always kinetic energy. A change from one type of energy to another is called a **conversion**.

Mechanical Energy

Mechanical energy is the term for the total potential and kinetic energy of an object. Another way to say that is with the equation:

$$mechanical\ energy = potential\ energy + kinetic\ energy$$

Mechanical energy can be increased by increasing either the potential energy, the kinetic energy, or both. For example, lifting a block or squishing a spring increases potential energy. In contrast, throwing a ball or swinging a hammer increases kinetic energy. In each of those examples, mechanical energy is increased.

Thermal Energy

Thermal energy is energy that is produced when particles move and give off **heat**. The Sun is the main source of the thermal energy on Earth. Fire is another natural source of thermal energy. Many devices, such as hair dryers, can also produce thermal energy using parts that are designed to heat up when they are powered using electrical energy.

Electrical Energy

Electrical energy is energy that is produced when **electrons** or **electric charges** move from one place to another. Items that need **electricity**, such as lights and household appliances, use electrical energy.

Light and Sound Energy

Light travels in waves, and the light visible to humans is an example of **light energy**. Most of the light energy on Earth comes from sunlight or bulbs powered by electricity.

Sound energy is caused by **vibrations**. When something moves or has an electrical current moving through it, it will vibrate. This creates waves that move through the space around the object that is vibrating, and sound energy is generated as those waves move. The way the vibration sounds depends on characteristics of the wave. Machines such as alarm clocks or radios include parts that are designed to produce sound waves.

Example

Which of these actions is an example of mechanical energy?

a. Warming your hands over a campfire
b. Using a lamp to read a book
c. Riding a bicycle
d. Listening to the radio

Choice A describes the transfer of heat from a fire to your hands. Heat is the movement of thermal energy, while mechanical energy is based on an object's motion or position. Choice A is not an example of mechanical energy.

Choice B involves a lamp, which converts electrical energy to produce light energy. Neither of these are examples of mechanical energy, so Choice B is not the answer.

Choice C involves someone applying a force to the pedals of a bicycle, causing the bicycle to move forward. Since mechanical energy has to do with the movement of an object, Choice C could be the answer.

Choice D describes a radio, which receives radio wave signals and converts them into sound energy. Sound energy does not involve the movement of an object, so Choice D is not the answer.

Choice C, riding a bicycle, is the only option that describes the energy of an object due to its motion or position, making it the correct answer.

Energy Source Examples

Energy exists in many forms and is defined by its ability to do work and cause change. Moving water and air are important sources of energy because their movement can produce electricity. Moving water produces energy based on how fast it moves, how far it falls, and how much water is flowing. Water is usually used to push turbine blades, which spin a generator to generate electricity. Wind turbines work similarly as the blades are pushed by the wind to turn a generator that produces electricity.

Energy Conversion

There are many examples of energy conversion, such as in an automobile. The **chemical energy** in the gasoline is converted to **mechanical energy** in the engine. Subsequently, this mechanical energy is converted to **kinetic energy** as the car moves. Additionally, the mechanical energy is converted to **electrical energy** to power the radio, headlights, air conditioner, and other devices. In the radio, electrical energy is converted to **sound energy**. In the headlights, it is converted to **heat** and **light energy**. In the air conditioner, it does work to remove heat energy from the car's interior. It is important to remember that, in all of these processes, a portion of the energy is lost from its intended purpose.

Examples of Energy Conversions

- Candles convert chemical energy to light and heat as they burn.
- Hydro-electric dams and wind turbines convert mechanical energy into electricity.
- The Sun uses nuclear energy to create heat and light.
- Light bulbs convert electrical energy into light and heat.
- Speakers convert electricity into sound energy.

Electrical Energy and Circuits

Electrical energy is the energy of small particles called **electrons** moving from one material to another. All matter has electrons, but some materials allow for their electrons to move more freely, which is why some materials are conductive and others are not. Just like with magnets, electricity can have a positive, negative, or neutral charge. Also like with magnets, **opposite charges attract**, whereas same charges repel each other, which is why clothes that are charged with static electricity cling to each other. Lightning is another good example of an electrical charge in nature. Lightning is made by friction between the air and the ground, which causes the ground to become positively charged and the clouds become negatively charged. These charges want to balance out, so when the charges become strong enough, they snap back together suddenly, creating a lightning bolt and causing the charges to neutralize.

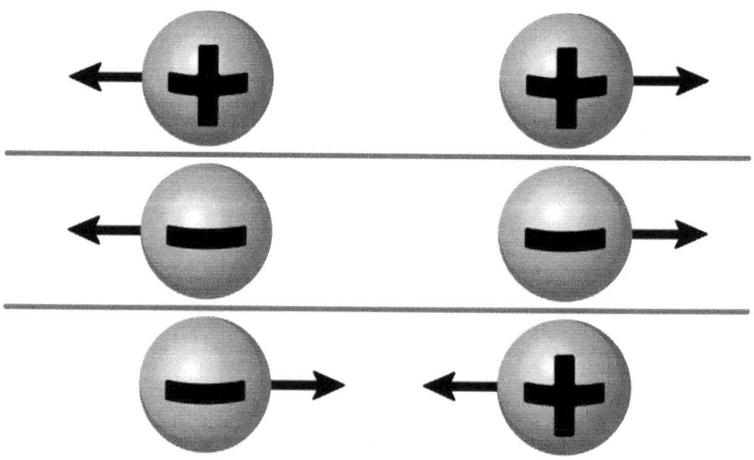

Circuits

Electricity does not flow on its own; there needs to be both an imbalance of negative and positive charges and there needs to be a path for the electrons to **flow** through. This path is called a **circuit**, and it is made of a conductive material, such as wire, that completes a full circle. A circuit also needs to have a **power source**, such as a battery, that pushes the electrical imbalance. When a circuit is complete, electrical energy will flow from positive to negative. The flow of electricity through a circuit is called a **current**. Current can flow through other objects, such as a light bulb, to use the energy without interrupting the circuit.

Parts in a Circuit

One of the most common parts in a circuit is a switch. To work, a circuit must have a continuous path for the electrical energy to flow through. A switch is simply a device that physically cuts the circuit so that the energy cannot flow. When the circuit is cut, there is no path for the energy to flow. Other common parts in circuits allow the current to flow through them, converting the energy into other forms. These objects are called **load objects** or **resistors**, and they include light bulbs and motors. Light bulbs convert the electrical energy into light, while motors convert the electrical energy into mechanical energy.

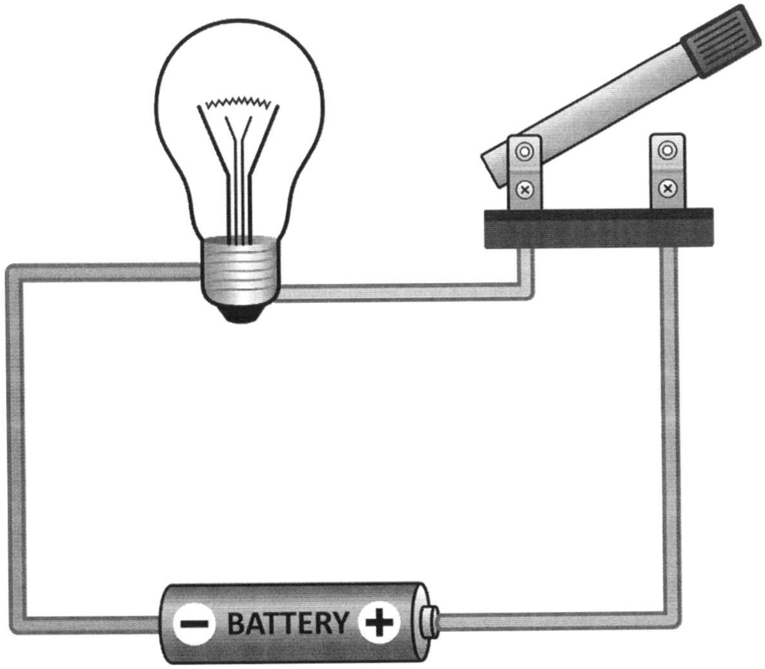

MAGNETISM

Magnetism is an **attraction** between opposite poles of **magnetic materials** and a **repulsion** between similar poles of magnetic materials. Magnetism can be natural or induced with the use of electric currents. Magnets almost always exist with two polar sides: north and south. A magnetic force exists between two poles on objects. Different poles attract each other. Like poles repel each other.

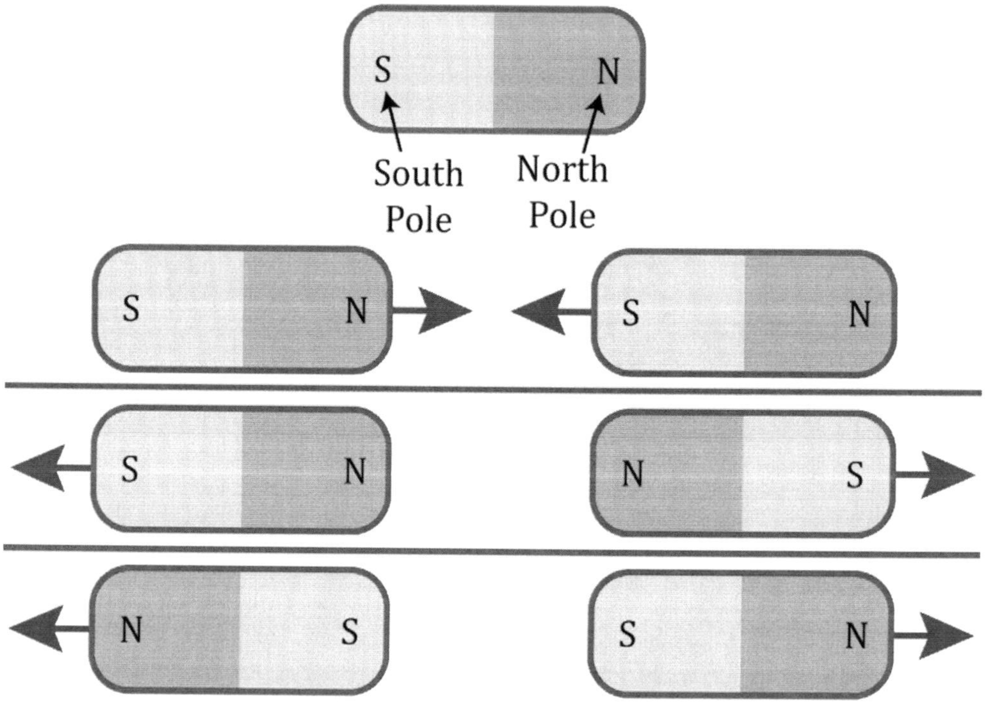

Heat

When two objects are rubbed together or an object rubs against another, heat, also known as thermal energy, is produced. This heat is produced because of friction, a force that opposes motion between two objects. The mechanical energy made from the movement of the objects becomes thermal energy. Friction explains why matches can create flames and why hands feel warmer after rubbing them together.

HEAT TRANSFER

Heat is a type of energy that is referred to as thermal energy. Heat transfers from the hot object to the cold object through the three forms of heat transfer: conduction, convection, and radiation.

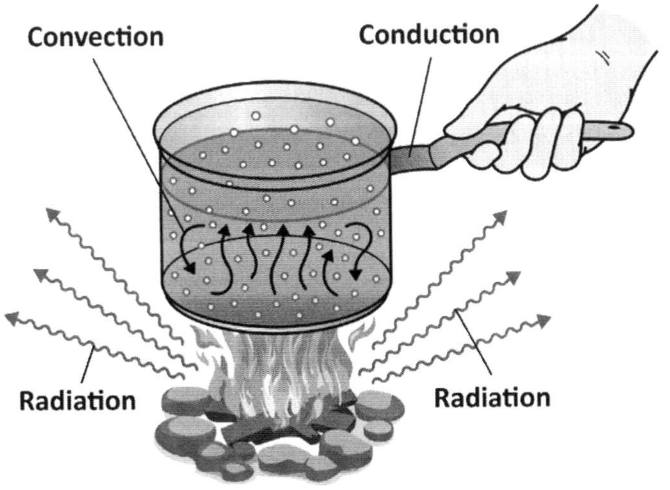

- **Conduction** is the transfer of heat by physical contact. When you touch a hot pot, the pot transfers heat to your hand by conduction.
- **Convection** is the transfer of heat by the movement of fluids. When you put your hand in steam, the steam transfers heat to your hand by convection.
- **Radiation** is the transfer of heat by electromagnetic waves. When you put your hand near a campfire, the fire heats your hand by radiation.

Review Video: Heat Transfer at the Molecular Level
Visit mometrix.com/academy and enter code: 451646

Conductors and Insulators

The terms conductor and insulator refer to how easily a material transfers energy to and from another material. Usually, this refers to **thermal** and **electrical** energy. A **conductor** is a material that easily transfers the energy, whereas an **insulator** does not easily transfer energy. Most materials that conduct heat well also conduct electricity well, and vice-versa. One example of a good conductor is copper wire. Copper wire is used in many electrical applications because it conducts electricity well. Most metals, like copper, also conduct heat well and are used in cooking because they heat up quickly and transfer the energy to the food that is being cooked. Examples of insulators include plastic, wood, and air.

CONDUCTORS AND INSULATORS USED TOGETHER

Insulators and conductors are often used together for better effect. For instance, the handle on a frying pan is usually made of silicone or plastic because it does not conduct heat well, whereas the rest of the pan is metal, which does conduct heat. The insulating properties of the plastic handle protect the cook's hand from being burned, while the metal parts of the pan help to cook the food. Insulators are also often used alongside conductors in electrical parts to help direct the flow of electricity and protect from shocks and fires. For instance, most outlets have a mixture of plastic parts and metal parts. The cover and the box that holds the outlet in the wall are usually plastic, and the wiring is covered with plastic to prevent shocks and fires, but the inside parts are usually made of copper, which help the electrical energy flow freely inside.

Examples of Conductors and Insulators

	Conductors	Insulators
Thermal	Aluminum, Copper, Silver, Diamonds	Plastic, Wood, Water, Air
Electrical	Gold, Steel, Copper, Water,	Rubber, Plastic, Glass, Rock, Wood, Air, Diamond

Properties of Light

Light is a type of **energy** that is on the **electromagnetic spectrum**. Light energy travels straight in one direction unless it touches another object that interferes with its path. Therefore, if a flashlight were turned on in space, the light could be seen on the other side of the galaxy, as long as it did not run into an object.

Light and Different Media

When talking about light, a **medium** is a substance through which light travels. There is no air in space, so there is no medium in space. This is why space is sometimes called a **vacuum**. On Earth, air and water are media through which light travels. Even though air is invisible, it slightly interferes with light. Air can cause light to **diffract**, or spread out. A flashlight does not shine in a perfectly straight line due to diffraction in air. Instead, it spreads out and gets weaker with distance from the light source.

Reflection

When light touches an object, it interacts in one of three ways. On shiny objects, such as mirrors, metal, and glass, at least some of the light energy **reflects**, causing it to suddenly change directions. The light's direction will be the opposite of its original angle.

REFRACTION

When light changes from one medium to another, the **frequency** of the light changes to match the new medium's **density**. Water is a different density than air, so when light enters water from the air, the angle of that light changes, which is called **refraction**. Because human vision is based on light, this produces an optical illusion when putting objects in water. If you were to insert a pencil into a cup of water, it would appear bent where the water starts.

ABSORPTION

Not all objects reflect well. When it touches an object that is not shiny, not much energy is reflected, but is instead **absorbed**. When light is absorbed, the type of energy is changed to **thermal energy**, causing a production of heat.

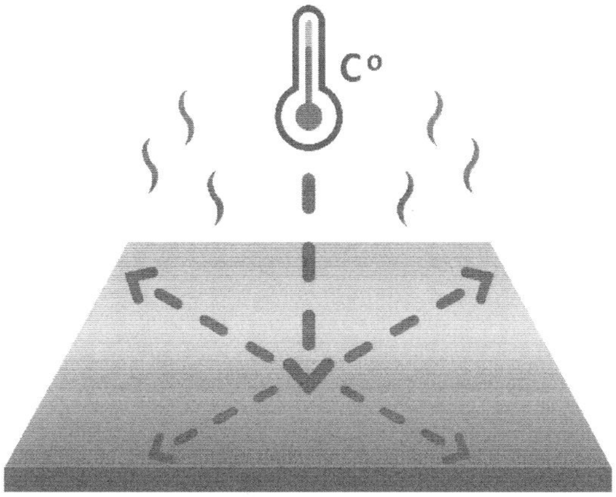

Sound Waves

The **pitch of a sound** as it reaches one's ear is based on the frequency of the sound waves. A high-pitched sound has a higher frequency than a low-pitched sound. Like all waves, sound waves transmit energy. The rate at which this energy is transmitted is the sonic power. Loudness, or intensity of sound, is the sonic power received per unit area.

When a pair of sound waves with slightly different frequencies interfere with one another causing a periodic variation in sound intensity or a **beat**. The frequency of the variation, called the **beat frequency**, is equal to the difference between frequencies of the two sound waves. The phenomenon is used when tuning two instruments to one another. As the two pitches get closer, the beat frequency will become smaller and smaller until it disappears entirely, indicating that the instruments are in tune.

Review Video: Sound
Visit mometrix.com/academy and enter code: 562378

Motion and Force

Sir Isaac Newton observed three major laws explaining how the motion of an object works. The term **motion** refers to the movement of an object and the term **force** refers to physical energy that is applied to an object. Newton also referred to objects that are not moving as being in a state of **rest**.

- **Newton's First Law of Motion** - a body will remain at **rest** or in **motion** until a **force** is applied to it.
  - A bowling ball continues to roll in the same direction it was thrown until friction eventually slows it down.
  - A ball sitting on the ground will not move unless a force is applied to it.

- **Newton's Second Law of Motion** -the amount of **acceleration** is determined by the amount of **force** and the **mass** of the object being moved.
  - A soccer ball will accelerate more if kicked harder.

  - A shopping cart is much easier to push than a car because it is much less massive.

- **Newton's Third Law of Motion** – For every **action**, there is an equal and opposite **reaction**.
  - The floor applies force upward to hold up the weight of a person standing on it.
  - A dog pulls against a leash that his owner is holding.

Directions of Motion

Motion can be either linear, rotational, or oscillating.

- **Linear motion** - a single direction, like a bowling ball rolling down the lane or a train moving in one direction down its tracks.
- **Rotational motion** – rotating or spinning in a circular motion, such as a top spinning, a merry-go-round, or the Earth rotating around the Sun.
- **Oscillating motion** – bouncing up and down repeatedly, such as a yo-yo on a string or a spring. This also includes waves as they rise and fall.

Mass and Strength of Force

An object with a large mass can be moved by strong forces, but may not be moved by a weak force. However, a weak force may move an object with little mass very easily. In general, a strong force will have a greater effect on an object than a weak force will.

Gravity

Gravity is a force that exists between all objects with matter. **Gravity** is a pulling force between objects, meaning that the forces on the objects point toward the opposite object. Gravity as we experience it is the force that the Earth exerts on objects, pulling them downward toward the center of the Earth. When Newton's third law is applied to gravity, the force pairs from gravity are shown to be equal in magnitude and opposite in direction.

Technically, all matter pulls other matter. The more massive the object, the more it pulls. The Earth is seen as our center of gravity because it is the most massive object nearby. Gravity is also reason that the Earth and other planets revolve around the Sun. The Sun is so massive that the Earth and all of the other bodies within the solar system are drawn to it and revolve around it as a result.

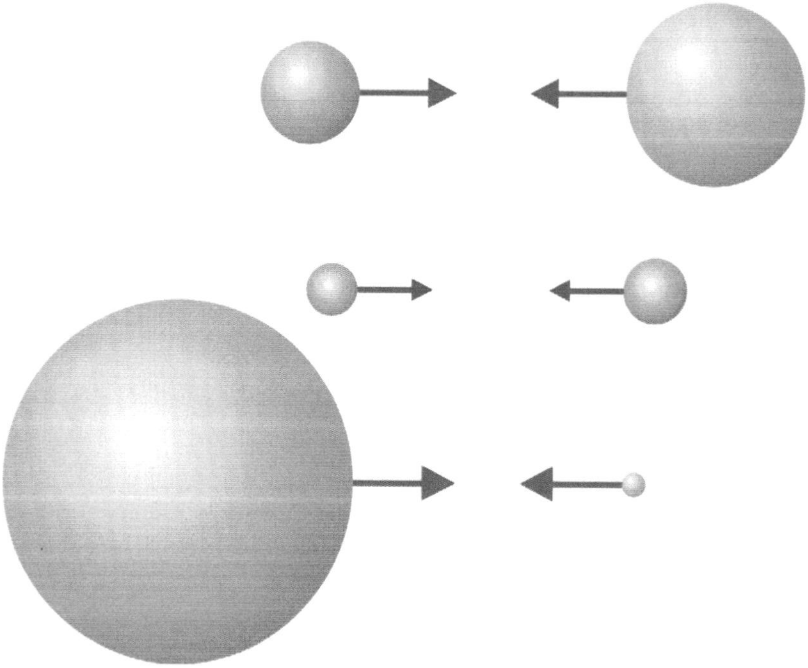

Forces Working Against Gravity

The direction of a force being applied to an object can impact the effect of the force. When force is applied to an object, it may be working against gravity. This means that the force must be **stronger** than gravity in order to move the object. If an object is on a flat surface, the pulling force used to lift it must be stronger than gravity, or the object will not be lifted. However, if an object is hanging from something, little force will be needed to pull it down because gravity is also working to pull it down. If an object is resting on an **incline**, gravity will be working to pull the object down the inclined surface. A pull from the higher side of the surface will not move the object unless it is stronger than gravity. Likewise, a push from the lower side of the surface will not move the object unless it is stronger than gravity. Objects on steeper inclines require more force to be moved.

FRICTION

Friction is a resistance to motion between contacting surfaces. In order to illustrate the concept of friction, let us imagine a book resting on a table. As it sits, the force of its weight is equal to and opposite of the normal force. If, however, we were to exert a force on the book, attempting to push it to one side, a frictional force would arise, equal and opposite to our force. This kind of frictional force is known as static frictional force.

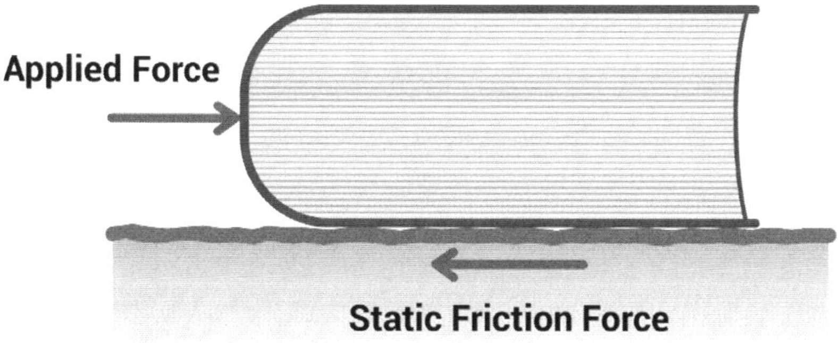

As we increase our force on the book, however, we will eventually cause it to accelerate in the direction of our force. At this point, the frictional force opposing us will be known as kinetic friction. For many combinations of surfaces, the magnitude of the kinetic frictional force is lower than that of the static frictional force, and consequently, the amount of force needed to maintain the movement of the book will be less than that needed to initiate the movement.

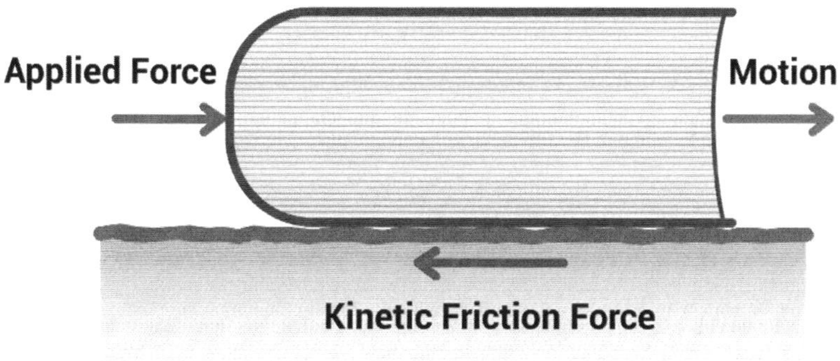

Review Video: Friction
Visit mometrix.com/academy and enter code: 716782

INERTIA, FRICTION, AND GRAVITY

When objects move, they keep moving until another force stops or changes its motion. This is called **inertia** or momentum. The heavier an object, the more inertia that object has. If there were no gravity or friction, an object in motion would go on moving in the same direction forever. In rotational motion, the mass of the object spinning has what is called rotational motion. Therefore, an object that is spinning, such as a spinning top, also carries momentum and would continue to spin forever if no other force were present. When a ball is rolled on the ground, the gravity of the Earth pulls the ball to the ground, which causes the ball to rub against the earth and cause friction. Instead of rolling forever, the friction slows the ball to a stop.

Speed

Speed measures the distance an object moves in a certain amount of time. For instance, if a car is moving at a speed of 65 miles per hour, then that car will travel 65 miles in one hour. To calculate average speed, you can divide the total distance traveled over the time that has passed: **speed = distance / time**. For example, consider the speed of a runner who runs an 800-meter race in 2 minutes. To calculate the runner's average speed, use the following formula:

speed = distance / time

800 meters / 2 minutes

400 m/min

When dividing two different units, such as meters and minutes, the units of the answer calculated will reflect the original units of the numerator and denominator. Example units for speed include miles per hour (mi/hr or mph), kilometers per hour (km/hr or km/h), or meters per second (m/s).

Balanced Forces

An object is in equilibrium when the sum of all forces acting on the object is zero. When the forces on an object sum to zero, the object does not accelerate. Equilibrium can be obtained when forces in the y-direction sum to zero, forces in the x-direction sum to zero, or forces in both directions sum to zero.

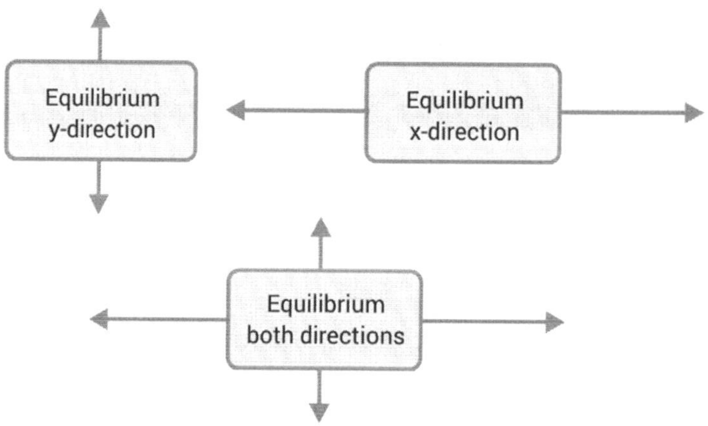

In most cases, a problem will provide one or more forces acting on an object and ask for a force to balance the system. The force will be the opposite of the current force or sum of current forces.

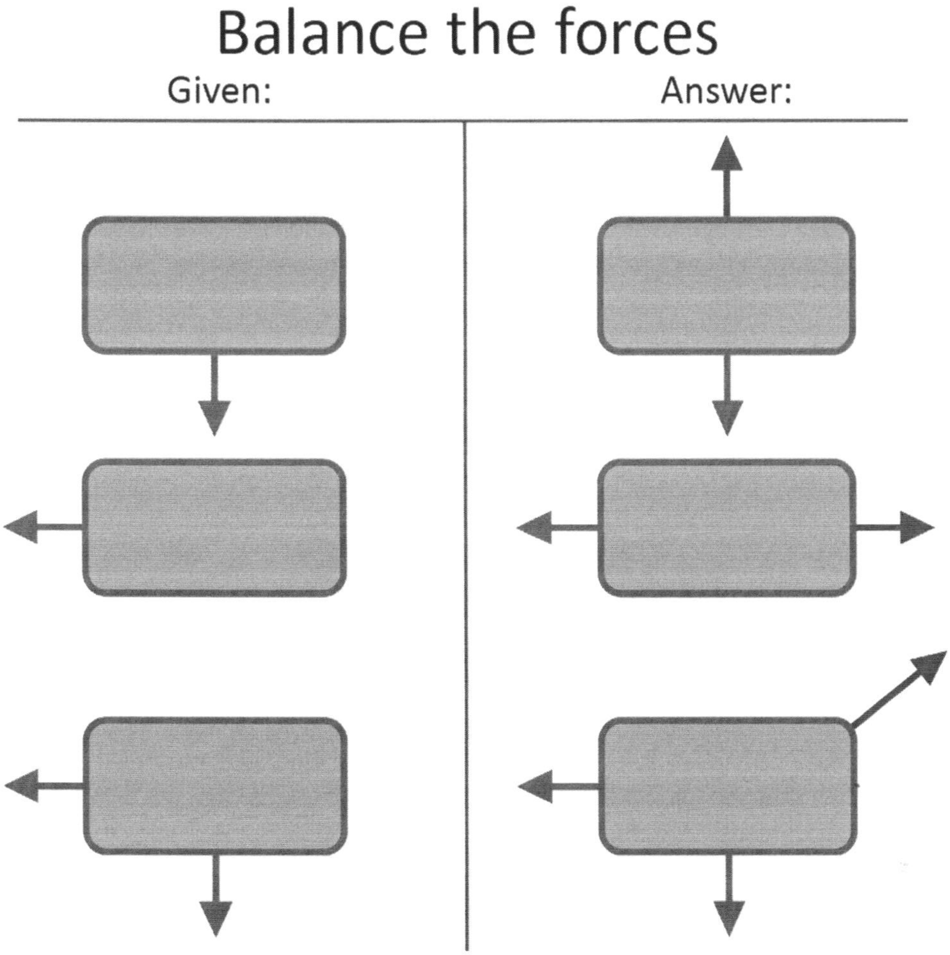

Chapter Quiz

1. Darla shined a flashlight on her bedroom wall as shown in the diagram below.

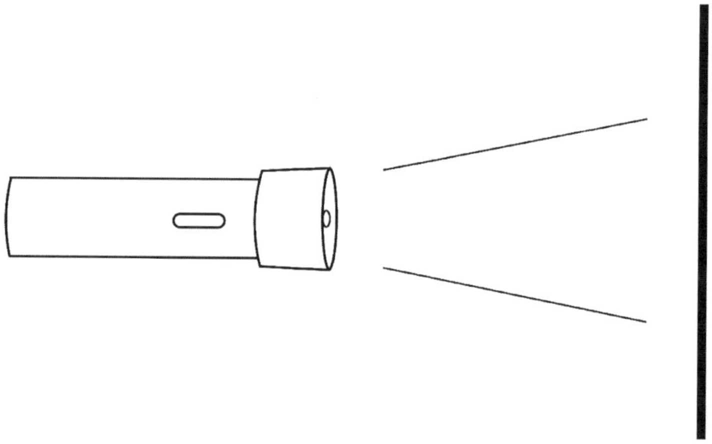

What property of light does this diagram illustrate?

a. Light travels in a straight line until its path is interrupted by another object.
b. Light is reflected when it hits another surface and changes direction.
c. Light is refracted when it moves through a liquid and is bent.
d. Light only travels a small distance before disappearing.

2. The diagrams below show light traveling through two different objects. Diagram 1 illustrates how light is reflected and Diagram 2 illustrates how light can be refracted.

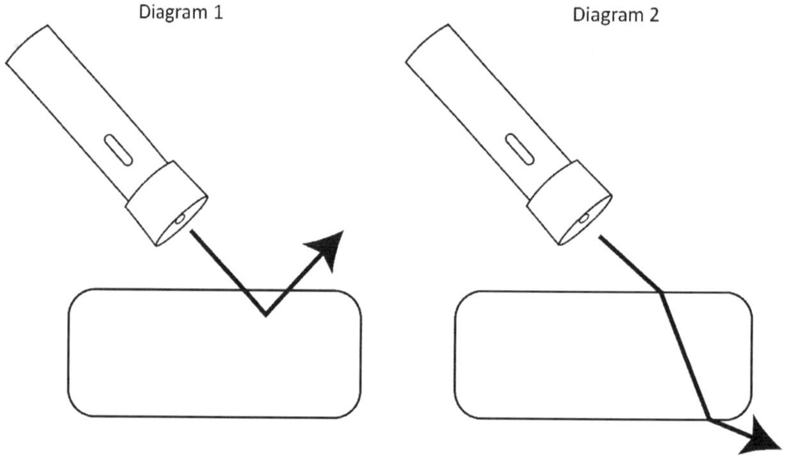

Students were asked to guess what the objects might be for each diagram. Which student's guess is most likely correct?

a. Student 1: The object in Diagram 1 could be a box and the object in Diagram 2 could be a window.
b. Student 2: The object in Diagram 1 could be a mirror and the object in Diagram 2 could be a glass of water.
c. Student 3: The object in Diagram 1 could be a wooden door and the object in Diagram 2 could be a chair.
d. Student 4: The object in Diagram 1 could be a glass jar and the object in Diagram 2 could be an umbrella.

3. While learning about the different sources of energy, Nelson took the notes shown below. However, he didn't hear the title for the second column.

Water Energy	________ Energy	Thermal Energy
White water rafting	Sailboat	Toaster
Dams	Turbine	Iron
Hydroelectric power plant	Kite	Hair dryer

Which source of energy belongs in the title for the second column?

a. Electric
b. Solar
c. Wind
d. Chemical

4. Which of the following explanations about electrically charged objects is false?

a. Objects with different electrical charges attract each other.
b. A balloon can attract another balloon if one is electrically charged and the other is not.
c. A charged object must be touching an uncharged object to attract it.
d. A balloon that is negatively charged will repel another balloon that is also negatively charged.

5. The science club worked to create circuits today. The four circuits they created are shown below.

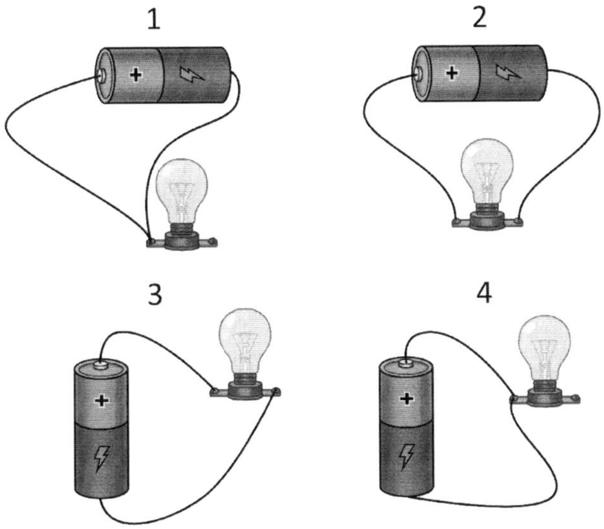

Which circuit(s) illustrate a closed circuit in which the light bulb would light up?

a. Circuit 1 and 2
b. Circuit 2 only
c. Circuits 2 and 3
d. Circuit 1 and 4

6. Students were asked to underline all the materials that are good conductors of electricity from a list of materials their teacher gave them. Which choice below shows all the materials on the list that should NOT be underlined?

Conductor or NOT?
Cooper
Steel
Wood
Gold
Plastic
Rubber
Aluminum
Glass

a. Copper, steel, gold, aluminum
b. Wood, gold, aluminum, glass
c. Wood, plastic, rubber, glass
d. Copper, wood, plastic, aluminum

7. A student takes the trash can to the curb every Tuesday and Thursday for trash collection. On Tuesday the trash container only had one trash bag inside. On Thursday, the trash container had five trash bags inside. Which statement describes a change that occurred on Thursday?

a. The force needed to move the trash container at the same speed will decrease from Tuesday to Thursday.
b. The force needed to move the trash container at the same speed will remain the same on Tuesday and Thursday.
c. The force needed to move the trash container at the same speed will increase from Tuesday to Thursday.
d. The force needed to move the box at the same speed will decrease and then increase on Thursday.

8. Olivia threw each of the items below using the same force of 20 Newtons. Which object traveled the shortest distance?

Object	Pushing Force	Mass	Object
Bouncy Ball	20 Newtons	38 grams	Bouncy Ball
Baseball	20 Newtons	145 grams	Baseball
Tennis Ball	20 Newtons	57.7 grams	Tennis Ball
Golf Ball	20 Newtons	45.9 grams	Golf Ball

a. Bouncy ball
b. Baseball
c. Tennis ball
d. Golf ball

9. Veronica made a snow globe last winter. She filled a clear jar with large sugar sprinkles and water and then glued a small snowman to the inside of the lid. She closed the jar, shook it up, and turned it over. The sugar sprinkles floated down to resemble snow. Twenty minutes later Veronica was disappointed to see that when she turned that jar over again, nothing fell from the top. What happened to the snow globe?

a. The sugar sprinkles attached to the snowman.
b. The sugar sprinkles dissolved in the water.
c. The sugar sprinkles sank to the bottom and leaked out of the jar.
d. The sugar sprinkles froze in the cold water.

10. How will the table picture below be expected to move?

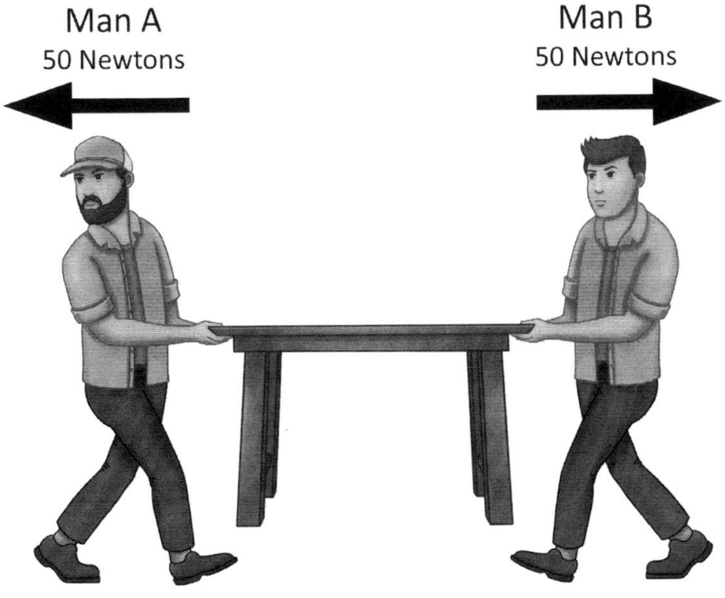

a. The table will move in the direction of Man A because he is pulling in that direction.
b. The table will move in the direction of Man B because he is pulling the table.
c. The table will not move because balanced forces are being applied in opposite directions.
d. The table will fall to the ground because the forces are equal.

Chapter Quiz Answers and Explanations

1. A: The diagram illustrates the principle that light will travel in a straight line until its path gets interrupted by another object. Light can be reflected or refracted like described, but that is not illustrated in the diagram. Light can travel large distances without stopping.

2. B: Student 2 is correct because light is reflected on surfaces like mirrors or shiny, smooth surfaces, and light is refracted when it travels through glass or water. The object in Diagram 1 cannot be a box or a wooden door since they do not have reflective properties. The object in Diagram 2 cannot be a chair or an umbrella because solids do not refract light.

3. C: A sailboat, turbine, and a kite all use the energy of the wind to operate correctly. These objects do not use energy from electricity, the sun, or chemical energy such as from battery sources.

4. C: A charged object does not have to be touching an uncharged object to attract it. The charged object can attract an uncharged object that is just near it. They do not have to be touching. Objects with different electrical charges do attract each other. A balloon that is electrically charged will attract another balloon that is not electrically charged. When both balloons have a negative charge, they will repel one another.

5. C: Circuits 2 and 3 both represent a closed circuit where the bulb will light because the conducting wires travel from the positive side of the power source to the bulb and from the negative side of the power source to the other side of the bulb. Circuits 1 and 4 have a conducting wire from both sides of the power source, but they each connect to the same side of the bulb, which is not a closed circuit.

6. C: Wood, plastic, rubber, and glass are not good conductors of electricity because electricity cannot flow easily through these objects. These objects do not have any free electrons that allow electricity to flow. Most metals such as copper, steel, gold, and aluminum are good conductors of electricity.

7. C: The mass of the trash container increased as more trash bags were added so more force will be needed to move the trash container at the same speed. The force needed to move the trash container will not decrease or remain the same because more trash bags were in the container, giving it a greater mass.

8. B: The baseball would travel the smallest distance. The greater the mass of the object, the less effect the force will have on the object, causing it not to travel as far as something with less mass. The bouncy ball, tennis ball, and golf ball would travel a greater distance with the same force because of their smaller amount of mass.

9. B: Sugar dissolves in water so the sugar sprinkles disappear after being in the water for a few minutes. The sugar would not attach to the snowman or leak out the bottom. The water would not be cold enough to cause the sugar sprinkles to freeze.

10. C: The table won't move. The same amount of force is being applied by both men, but in opposite directions. This creates a balanced force which will not result in movement. Man A is pulling the table in his direction, but Man B is pulling with the same force in the opposite direction so the table will not move toward either man. When forces are equal, the object won't move, and a force would have to stop for it to fall to the ground.

Life Science

Human Anatomy

Tissues

Tissues are groups of cells that work together to perform a specific function. Tissues can be grouped into four broad categories: muscle tissue, connective tissue, nerve tissue, and epithelial tissue. Muscle tissue is involved in body movement. **Muscle tissues** can be composed of skeletal muscle cells, cardiac muscle cells, or smooth muscle cells. Skeletal muscles include the muscles commonly called biceps, triceps, hamstrings, and quadriceps. Cardiac muscle tissue is found only in the heart. Smooth muscle tissue provides tension in the blood vessels, controls pupil dilation, and aids in peristalsis. **Connective tissues** include bone tissue, cartilage, tendons, ligaments, fat, blood, and lymph. **Nerve tissue** is located in the brain, spinal cord, and nerves. **Epithelial tissue** makes up the layers of the skin and various membranes. Tissues are grouped together as organs to perform specific functions.

Organ Systems

Organs are groups of tissues that work together to perform specific functions. **Organ systems** are groups of organs that work together to perform specific functions. Complex animals have several organs that are grouped together in multiple systems. In mammals, there are 11 major organ systems: integumentary system, respiratory system, circulatory system, endocrine system, nervous system, digestive system, excretory system, muscular system, skeletal system, reproductive system, and immune system.

1. **Integumentary system:** the protective barrier of the body, including skin, hair, and nails.
2. **Respiratory system:** responsible for allowing air to enter and exit the lungs to obtain oxygen and release carbon dioxide. The respiratory system consists of the nasal passages, pharynx, larynx, trachea, bronchial tubes, lungs, and diaphragm.
3. **Circulatory system:** includes the heart, blood, and blood vessels that carry blood through the body, delivering oxygen to tissues.
4. **Endocrine system:** manages and releases hormones responsible for bodily functions and behavior, including hunger, stress, sleep, and many others. The endocrine system consists of several ductless glands, which secrete hormones directly into the bloodstream.
5. **Nervous system:** includes your brain, spinal cord, sense organs, and nerves. The nervous system allows you to sense, process, and respond to external stimuli. It also helps regulate physiological and behavioral processes.
6. **Digestive system:** processes and extracts nutrients from food. The excretory system is responsible for removing waste following digestion. The digestive system includes the stomach, intestines, liver, gallbladder, pancreas, and anus.
7. **Excretory system:** metabolizes food, filters blood, and excretes waste. It includes the kidneys and bladder.
8. **Muscular system:** includes muscles that allow the body to move. The muscles work in combination with the skeletal system.
9. **Skeletal system:** includes the bones, joints, and cartilage that make up your skeleton.
10. **Reproductive system:** enables humans to produce offspring. It includes the external and internal reproductive organs.

11. **Immune System:** keeps a record of microbes to recognize and destroy the microbes that enter your body and make you feel sick. It includes white blood cells, antibodies, complement system, lymphatic system, spleen, bone marrow, and thymus.

Genetics and Heredity

Genetics is the study of biological inheritance in organisms. Animals generally reproduce with a mother and a father, which both contribute their **genetic** information to offspring. The passing along of genetic traits is also known as **heredity**. The offspring of a mother with red hair and blue eyes with a father who has brown hair and brown eyes may receive any combination of those traits. Another example may be a red fox mating with a brown fox; the offspring may have either brown fur or red fur, and a pack of siblings may have a mixture of inherited traits. This type of inheritance can also be seen in plant life, as pink and white flowered plants may breed together to produce either pink or white flowered offspring, or even special hybrids with blended colors.

Modes of Reproduction

Animals can reproduce sexually or asexually. Most animals reproduce sexually. In **sexual reproduction**, males and females have different reproductive organs that produce **gametes**. Males have testes that produce sperm, and females have ovaries that produce eggs. During fertilization, a sperm cell unites with an egg cell, forming a **zygote**. Fertilization can occur internally such as in most mammals and birds or externally such as aquatic animals such as fish and frogs. The zygote undergoes cell division, which develops into an embryo and eventually develops into an adult organism. Some embryos develop in eggs such as in fish, amphibians, reptiles, and birds. Some mammals are **oviparous** meaning that they lay eggs, but most are **viviparous** meaning they have a uterus in which the embryo develops. One particular type of mammal called **marsupials** give birth to an immature fetus that finishes development in a pouch. However, there are some animals reproduce **asexually**. For example, hydras reproduce by budding, and starfish and planarians can reproduce by fragmentation and regeneration. Some fish, frogs, and insects can even reproduce by parthenogenesis, which is a type of self-reproduction without fertilization.

Effects of the Modes of Reproduction on Offspring

With **asexual reproduction**, an organism provides all of the **genes** to its offspring, making it like a **clone**, or exactly like the parent in its genetic makeup. This means that the offspring will be very similar to the parent unless there is a random mutation that causes a change. This means that the offspring will be very uniform to each other. In **sexual reproduction**, both parents provide genetic information that can be inherited, causing much more variety in the offspring from generation to generation. This more aggressive variation means that natural selection and adaptation is more likely to make a difference for the species in the long-term.

Review Video: Asexual Reproduction
Visit mometrix.com/academy and enter code: 565616

Due to mutations over long periods, genes come in alternate forms, called **alleles**, that determine how a **trait** will be represented in the offspring. Different alleles govern many different traits. Sexual reproduction makes new combinations of existing alleles. These new combinations lead to variations in physical and behavioral traits that lead to adaptation and selection, which are key components of evolution.

Producers, Consumers, and Decomposers

Producers are organisms that can make their own food. Most producers are plants. Plants use sunlight, carbon dioxide from the air, and water to make sugars that provide **energy** through a process called **photosythesis**. Plants only need sunlight, water, and certain minerals and other nutrients to live, grow, and reproduce. **Consumers** are organisms that eat other organisms. **Decomposers** are organisms that feed on decaying plant and animal matter. Since decomposers cannot make their own food, they are classified as consumers. Fungi, such as mushrooms, are decomposers. They break down the tissues and wood of living or dead plants or the bodies of dead animals.

Energy Pyramid

Energy flows through an ecosystem as producers and consumers are consumed by other organisms. The flow of energy can be tracked through an energy pyramid. An **energy pyramid** shows how energy is transferred from one trophic level to another. **Trophic levels** describe whether an organism is a producer or a consumer and how much energy is typically passed to them when they eat. Producers always form the **base** of an energy pyramid, and the energy they pass along comes from the **Sun**. Consumers form successive levels above the producers. Producers only store about 1% of the solar energy they receive. Then, each successive level only uses about 10% of the energy of the previous level. Therefore, **primary consumers** use about 10% of the energy used by primary producers, such as grasses and trees. Next, **secondary consumers** use 10% of the energy used by primary consumers, or 1% overall. This continues up for as many trophic levels as exist in a particular ecosystem.

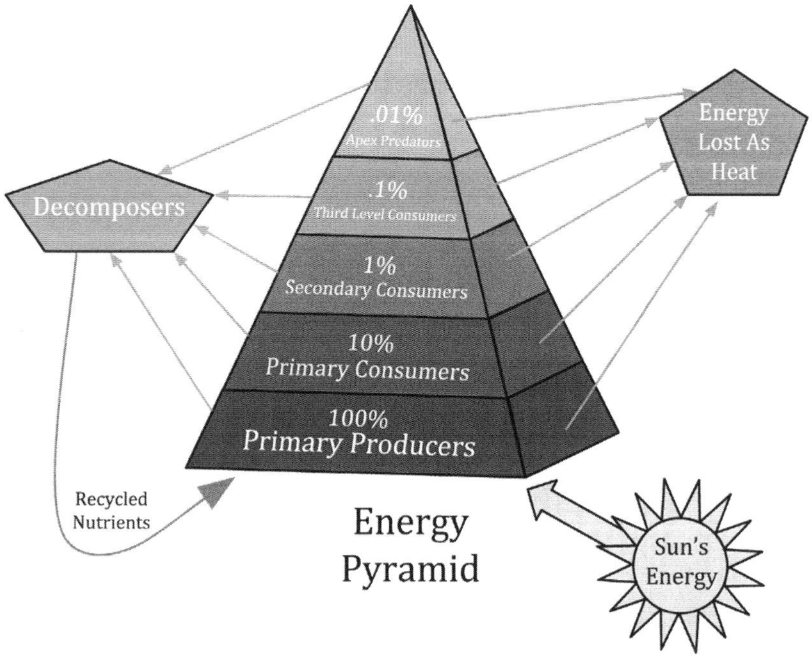

Food Web

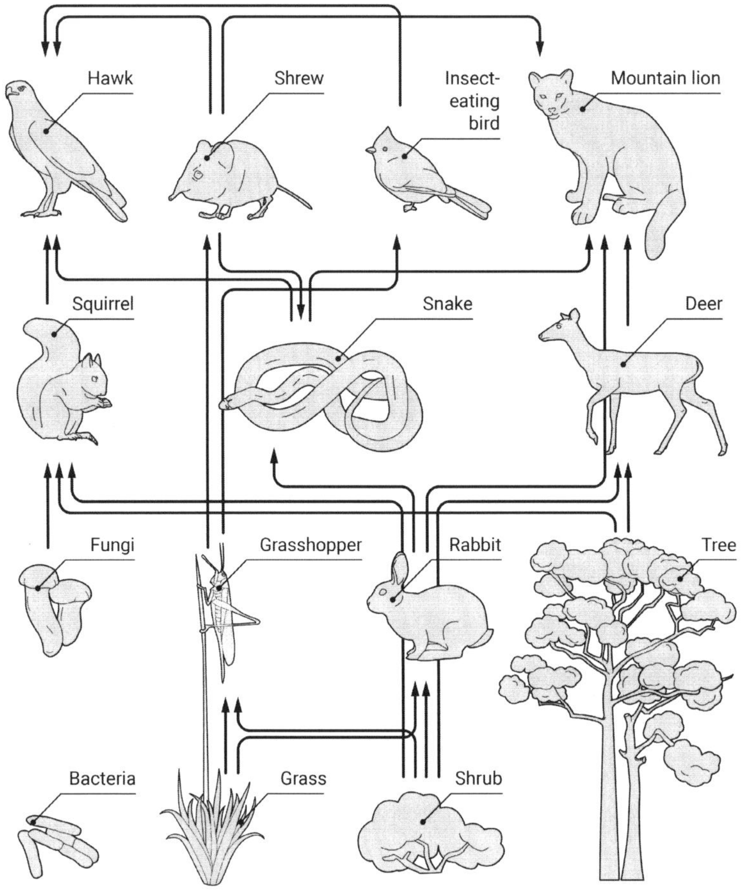

Energy flow through an ecosystem can also be illustrated by a **food web**. Energy moves through the food web in the direction of the arrows. In the food web above, **producers** such as grass, trees, and shrubs use energy from the Sun to produce food through photosynthesis. **Herbivores** or **primary consumers** such as squirrels, grasshoppers, and rabbits obtain energy by eating producers. **Secondary consumers**, which are carnivores such as snakes and shrews, obtain energy by eating the primary consumers. **Tertiary consumers**, which are carnivores such as hawks and mountain lions, obtain energy by eating the secondary consumers.

Review Video: Food Webs
Visit mometrix.com/academy and enter code: 853254

Interdependence of the Food Web

Because each level of consumer is dependent on the previous level for food, the population of each level affects the other animal groups. For instance, if an ecosystem is made up of only grass, deer, and wolves, grass is the producer, the deer eat the grass, and the wolves eat the deer. If deer are overhunted one year, the grass is given more room to grow because less of it is consumed. However, the wolves will not have enough food, so the wolf population will reduce in size. Eventually, because of the abundance of grass and a reduced population of wolves, the deer may then have a surge in population the next year. This example is not a realistic example, as there are usually many more producers, consumers, and predators within an ecosystem.

EXAMPLE

Which of the following accurately depicts the first three steps in the movement of energy through an ecosystem?

a. Sun → producers → consumers
b. Producers → Sun → consumers
c. Consumers → producers → decomposers
d. Decomposers → consumers → producers

Choice A depicts the movement of energy from the Sun to producers and then to consumers. Producers get energy from the Sun through photosynthesis, while consumers get energy by eating plants or other animals. The path depicted in Choice A matches this pattern, so Choice A could be the correct answer.

Choice B depicts energy moving from producers to the Sun and then to consumers. Producers such as plants gain energy from the Sun, so the Sun should come first in this pathway. Choice B is incorrect.

Choice C describes the movement of energy from consumers to producers and then to decomposers. Producers get energy from the Sun while consumers eat other living organisms, so producers should always come before consumers in an energy pathway. Choice C is not the answer.

Choice D depicts the movement of energy from decomposers to consumers and then to producers. Decomposers get energy by breaking down the remains of plants and animals that have died, recycling nutrients into the ecosystem. Decomposers cannot be the first step in energy transfer, so Choice D is incorrect.

Choice A is the correct answer because it accurately shows the movement of energy from the Sun to producers through photosynthesis, followed by consumers that eat other living organisms.

FOOD WEB IN A POND

Sunlight allows green algae to photosynthesize and grow. The algae are fed upon by small animals like water fleas and copepods. In turn, these are eaten by small worms, mosquito larvae and other larval insects. These are then eaten by mosquito fish, which in turn are eaten by larger fishes like bluegills. The bluegills are preyed upon by even larger fishes like bass and by herons, egrets and raccoons (which also eat the bass). Then the animal waste and everything that dies and settles to the bottom is decomposed by bacteria and fungi.

FOOD WEB IN A MEADOW

Sunlight allows grass and other plants to grow. These plants are eaten by a variety of *herbivores* like insects, rodents, and rabbits. Their seeds are consumed by various birds such as sparrows and quail. The insects are eaten by *carnivores*, including other kinds of birds, shrews, and bats. The rodents, rabbits, and some of the birds are then eaten by larger carnivores like weasels and foxes. Also, the quail, mice, rabbits and shrews are eaten by owls at night and by hawks during the day.

Plants

Plants are multicellular organisms with eukaryotic cells containing cellulose in their cell walls. Plant cells have chlorophyll and perform photosynthesis. Plants can be vascular or nonvascular. **Vascular plants** have true leaves, stems, and roots that contain xylem and phloem. **Nonvascular plants** lack true leaves, stems and roots and do not have any true vascular tissue but instead rely on diffusion and osmosis to transport most of materials or resources needed to survive. Almost all plants are autotrophic, relying on photosynthesis for food. A small number do not have chlorophyll and are parasitic, but these are extremely rare. Plants can reproduce sexually or asexually. Many plants reproduce by seeds produced in the fruits of the plants, while some plants reproduce by seeds on cones. One type of plant, ferns, reproduce by a different system that utilizes spores. Some plants can even reproduce asexually by vegetative reproduction.

Major Plant Processes

There are three key processes that plants need to survive: photosynthesis, respiration, and transpiration. **Photosynthesis** is the process that plants use to create food. Photosynthesis requires water, carbon dioxide, and sunlight. Photosynthesis creates glucose molecules that can be broken down and used as energy for the plant. The cellular **respiration** process breaks glucose molecules into usable energy for the cell. Respiration requires oxygen to take place, so the plants take in oxygen. **Transpiration** is the process of plants losing water through their leaves. Plants can control the amount of water lost through their leaves. Water is lost through stomata on the underside of the leaves. Stomata can be opened and closed by guard cells.

Plant Life Cycles and Reproductive Strategies

Pollination Strategies

Pollination is the transfer of pollen from the anther of the stamen to the stigma of the pistil on the same plant or on a different plant. Pollinators can be either **abiotic** (not derived from a living organism) or **biotic** (derived from a living organism). Abiotic pollinators include wind and water. Approximately 20% of pollination occurs by abiotic pollinators. For example, grasses are typically pollinated by wind, and aquatic plants are typically pollinated by water. Biotic pollinators include insects, birds, mammals, and occasionally reptiles. Most biotic pollinators are insects. Many plants have colored petals and strong scents, which attract insects. Pollen rubs off on the insects and is transferred as they move from plant to plant.

Seed Dispersal Methods

Methods of **seed dispersal** can be abiotic or biotic. Methods of seed dispersal include gravity, wind, water, and animals. Some plants produce seeds in fruits that get eaten by animals and then are distributed to new locations in the animals' waste. Some seeds (e.g. dandelions) have structures to aid in dispersal by wind. Some seeds have barbs that get caught in animal hair or bird feathers and are then carried to new locations by the animals. Interestingly, some animals bury seeds for food storage but do not return for the seeds. The seeds of aquatic plants can be dispersed by water, while the seeds of plants near rivers, streams, lakes, and beaches (e.g. coconuts) are also often dispersed by water. Some plants, in a method called **mechanical dispersal**, can propel or shoot their seeds away from them even up to several feet. For example, touch-me-nots and violets utilize mechanical dispersal.

Alternation of Generations

Alternation of generations, also referred to as **metagenesis**, contains both a sexual phase and an asexual phase in the life cycle of the plant. Mosses and ferns reproduce by alternation of generations: the sexual phase is called the **gametophyte**, and the asexual phase is called the

sporophyte. During the sexual phase, a sperm fertilizes an egg to form a zygote. By mitosis, the zygote develops into the sporophyte. The sporangia in the sori of the sporophyte produce the spores through meiosis. The spores germinate and by mitosis produce the gametophyte.

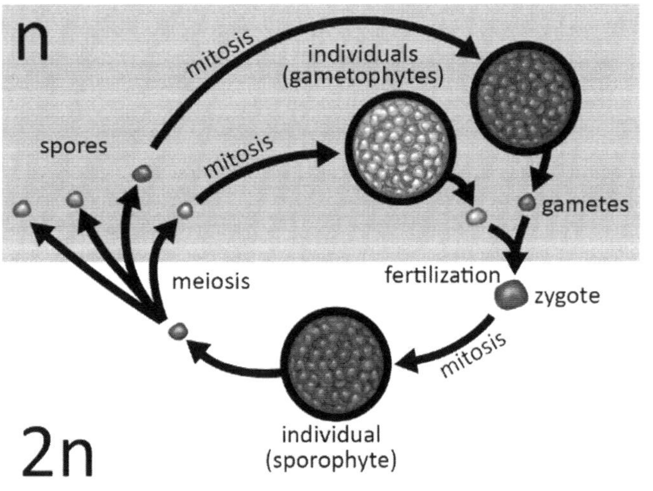

Plant Species Competing with Each Other

Creosote bush is the most widespread shrub in the deserts of the American Southwest where water can be very scarce for long periods. The roots of mature creosote bushes are extremely efficient and absorb all the water in the sandy soil around them. This creates very dry zones around each plant. The seeds of other plants cannot survive long enough to germinate. Therefore, the plants tend to be spaced far apart from each other.

Effects of Temperature, Light, Moisture, and Air on Plant Growth

Environmental factors including temperature, light, moisture, and air can all impact plant growth. **Temperature** is the most important environmental factor determining plant growth. The temperature needs vary for different plants. Tender plants will not grow in cold conditions. Plants use photosynthesis to create food. For photosynthesis to take place, plants need **light**. Without light, plants cannot produce food and will die. Water is essential for all life, including plants. **Water** is the main component of plant cells and helps keep the plant turgid. A plant without water will wilt and die. Water is required in photosynthesis and is used to transport nutrients in the plant. **Air** is required for both the production of food (photosynthesis) and the breakdown of food into energy (respiration).

Flowering Versus Nonflowering Plants

Angiosperms and gymnosperms are both vascular plants. **Angiosperms** are flowering plants, and **gymnosperms** are non-flowering plants. Angiosperms reproduce by seeds that are enclosed in an ovary, usually in a fruit, while gymnosperms reproduce by unenclosed or "naked" seeds, referred to as spores, on scales, leaves, or cones. Angiosperms can be further classified as either monocots or dicots, depending on if they have one or two cotyledons, respectively. Angiosperms include grasses, garden flowers, vegetables, and broadleaf trees such as maples, birches, elms, and oaks. Gymnosperms include conifers such as pines, spruces, cedars, and redwoods. Ferns and mosses are also known for producing spores for reproduction.

Review Video: Kingdom Plantae Characteristics
Visit mometrix.com/academy and enter code: 710084

Types of Animals

VERTEBRATE

A *vertebrate* is an animal with an internal *spinal column* (backbone) composed of soft cartilage or hard bone. Vertebrates also have a skull which contains a brain and most have paired *appendages* (legs, flippers or fins). Lampreys, sharks and rays, bony fishes, amphibians (frogs and salamanders), reptiles, birds and mammals are all vertebrates. Image by Ruth Lawson Otago Polytechnic.

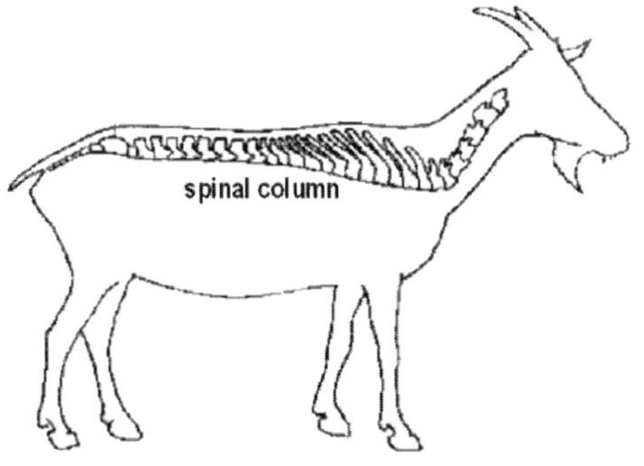

INVERTEBRATE

Invertebrates lack an internal spinal column. Their shape is maintained by a hard, rigid outer shell or covering called an exoskeleton or by the pressure of their internal fluids (like a plastic bag full of water). Insects, spiders, centipedes, snails, clams, octopuses and squids, and earthworms are all invertebrates.

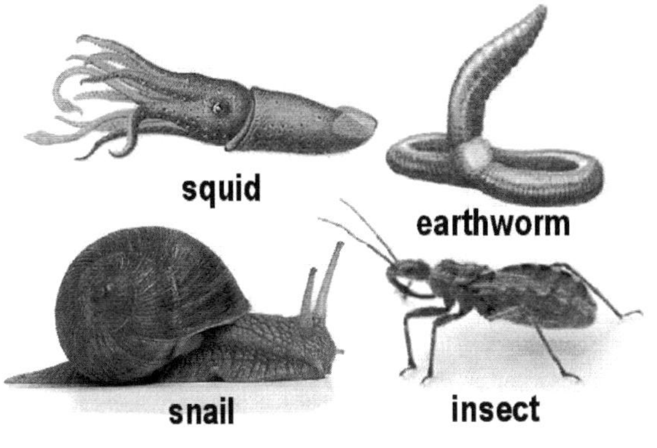

MAMMALS

Mammals are air-breathing, warm-blooded vertebrates with a backbone, skull, internal skeleton and a well-developed brain. Most are covered with hair, and most have specialized teeth. Most give birth to live young, and the mothers produce milk to nourish their young. Birds are also warm-blooded, but they are covered with feathers instead of hair, their young hatch from hard-shelled eggs, and they have no teeth. Bats, platypuses, opossums, kangaroos, elephants, deer, squirrels, apes, monkeys, and whales are all mammals.

REPTILE

Reptiles are air-breathing vertebrates. They cannot generate their own body heat like mammals and birds. Their skin is covered with scales or horny plates. Some lay eggs on land, and others have eggs that hatch inside the mother, and the young are born live. Crocodiles and alligators, turtles, lizards and snakes (like the cobra shown here) are all reptiles. Other reptiles include the dinosaurs, ichthyosaurs, and flying reptiles that died out millions of years ago.

AMPHIBIAN

Amphibians are cold-blooded, air-breathing vertebrates with a smooth and slimy or dry and warty skin. Most lay their eggs in water, but a few lay eggs in wet areas on land. Unlike reptiles and birds, amphibian eggs lack any kind of protective outer shell. Many amphibians undergo metamorphosis from a gill-breathing tadpole stage to an air-breathing adult. Frogs, toads, and salamanders are all amphibians.

FROGS

Frogs are *amphibians*. That means they must lay their eggs in water. The egg cell divides to form an *embryo* that grows until it begins to look like a *tadpole* (Fig. 1). Eventually the tadpole swims freely in the water and breathes with gills. As the tadpole develops it grows one hind leg (Fig. 2), then another (Fig. 3), and finally 2 front legs (Fig. 4). The tail shrinks (Fig. 5) until it disappears and the tadpole has *metamorphosed* into a tiny *frog*.

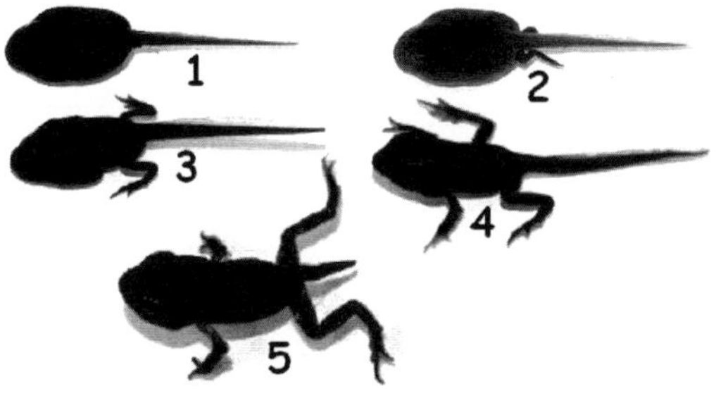

To a scientist there is very little difference between a frog and a toad. All toads are really just frogs. But for most people, a frog usually refers to a tailless amphibian that lives entirely or mostly in or around water and has smooth slimy skin. A toad, on the other hand, has dry, warty skin and lives on land away from water. But both lay their eggs in water, and their tadpoles develop in water.

FISH

Except for lungfish, fishes are gill-breathing animals with a backbone, skull and internal skeleton that live in the water (although some can come out on land for short periods). They have no legs, but most have paired fins for swimming. Most are cold-blooded, although a few fast swimmers can raise their body temperature slightly. They lay their eggs in the water. Sharks, bass, tuna, salmon, goldfish, and catfish are all different types of fishes.

SHARK, DOLPHIN, AND PORPOISE

Sharks are a type of fish and breathe by means of gills. Although they look somewhat the same, dolphins and porpoises are mammals that live in the ocean. They breathe by means of lungs, and they must come to the surface to take in air through blowholes on top of their heads. Sharks swim by moving their vertical tails from side to side. Dolphins move their horizontal flukes up and down.

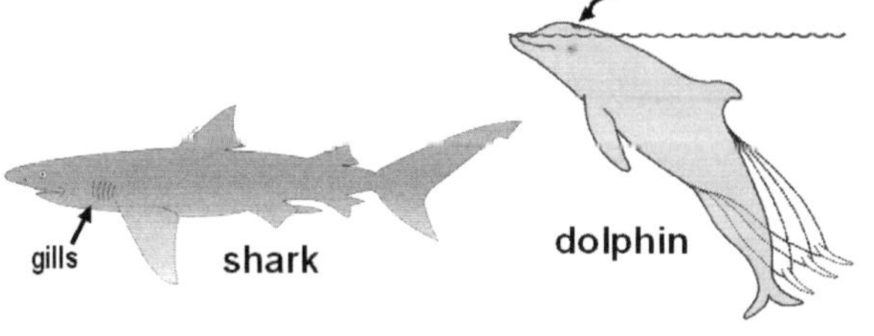

INSECTS

Insects are *arthropods* (joint-legged animals) whose bodies are divided into three parts: a head, thorax, and abdomen. Insects all have a hard outer covering called an *exoskeleton*, three pairs of legs (6 in all), compound eyes, and a single pair of antennae. They have to molt and shed their hard outer skin in order to grow. More than half of all living animals are insects. Spiders, scorpions, centipedes and millipedes are not insects but belong to different groups of arthropods.

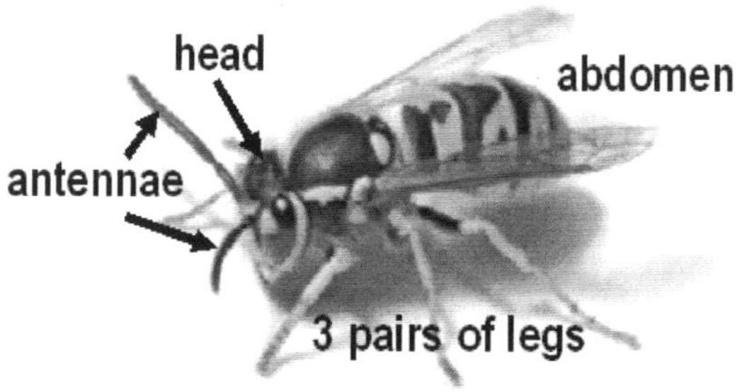

FIREFLIES

Fireflies or "lightning bugs" are actually flying beetles that come out at night. They have special light producing organs in their bellies that create a cold form of biological light. They flash their light on and off in a pattern unique to each species in order to attract a mate. Females of some predatory species of firefly imitate the flashing pattern of the females of a different species to attract the male. When the male of the other species approaches, she kills and eats him.

SPIDERS AND SCORPIONS

Spiders and scorpions are not insects, but arachnids. Spiders and scorpions have four pairs of walking legs, simple (not compound) eyes, and no antennae. The body is divided into two parts: a cephalothorax (the fused head and thorax) and an abdomen.

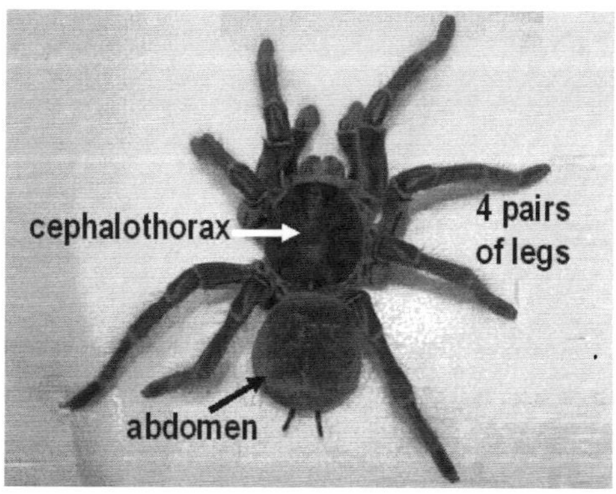

SPIDER WEBS

Most spiders produce silk from glands at the tip of their abdomen. These glands can produce a trailing safety line and sticky silk making a web to trap their prey. An orb web like the one shown here lets the spider sit and wait for prey to be caught in the sticky web. This web helps the spider save energy since it does not have to hunt and chase down its prey like some spiders do. Weight for weight, spider silk is stronger than steel.

MILLIPEDE

Millipedes and centipedes are not insects. Millipedes and insects are both arthropods, but that is where the similarities end. Millipedes are called *myriapods.* Millipedes have 1 pair of antennae, but only simple eyes called *ocelli.* They have a head, a great many body segments, and *two pairs of legs* on most segments. Most eat dead plant matter. Insects have a pair of antennae, but they have compound eyes, a head, thorax, and abdomen, and just three pairs of legs.

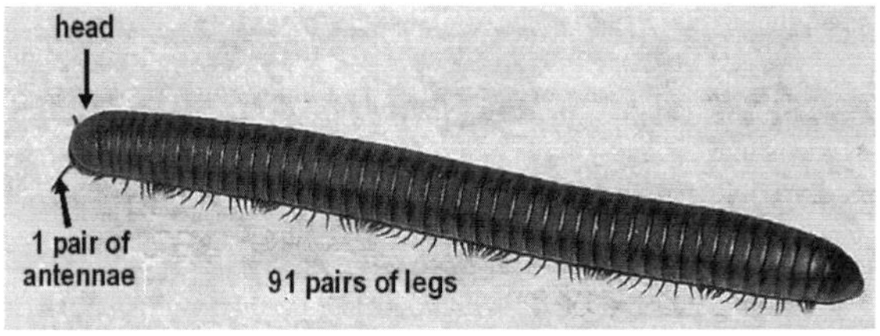

Centipedes are called *chilopods.* They have a pair of antennae, many body segments, and *a single pair of legs* on each segment. Centipedes are carnivorous and have a pair of fangs formed from their first legs that they use to inject venom into their prey. Insects have a pair of antennae, but they have compound eyes, a head, thorax, and abdomen, and just three pairs of legs.

HERBIVORES, CARNIVORES, AND OMNIVORES

Herbivores are animals that only eat plants. Examples are rabbits, deer, antelope, rhinoceroses and elephants. **Carnivores** are animals that only eat other animals, like lions, wolves, foxes, most bats, hawks and owls, insect-eating birds, snakes, and sharks. **Omnivores** are animals that eat both plants and other animals. Examples include bears, pigs, skunks, raccoons, birds like crows and ravens, and human beings.

Vultures

Vultures are mostly **scavengers** that eat *carrion*— the dead and decaying flesh of animals. When an animal dies it immediately begins to decay or rot. Bacteria break down the dead tissues and release a foul smell that attracts scavengers like vultures, hyenas, crabs and lobsters, and certain flies that feed on decaying flesh. Many carnivores like coyotes, hyenas, opossums, hawks and eagles will also eat carrion in addition to catching live prey.

Populations of Animals or Plants

A population consists of all of the organisms of a certain kind in a defined area, region, or habitat. It may be all the red foxes in a given national park, all the loblolly pines in Virginia (very hard to count), all the bullfrogs in a certain pond, or even all of the boxelder bugs on a single box elder tree. In the case of rare or endangered species it may be all of the individuals still living in the wild.

Several factors operate to keep animal and plant populations under control. Predation, grazing, disease, competition for limiting resources such as food or nutrients, water, habitat and living space, hunting and breeding territory, and sunlight for plants all play important roles. Even the size of the population can influence factors such as birth rate and severity of disease outbreaks or force individuals to migrate to other less crowded areas.

Changes Throughout the Life Cycle

Many types of plants and animals go through a process of changes throughout their lifespans. This process often involves a complete change in how the plant or animal looks and acts during that life stage. In insects and in amphibians, this is called **metamorphosis**.

Complete Versus Incomplete Metamorphosis

For example, the eastern lubber grasshopper undergoes incomplete metamorphosis. This means it starts as an egg, grows into a nymph or adolescent, and then becomes an adult. The cardinal ladybird, on the other hand, undergoes complete metamorphosis. This means it starts as an egg, then turns into a larva, then turns to a pupa, and last it turns to an adult. The life cycle of many larger animals is similar to complete metamorphosis as they start as an egg, grow into an embryo, then a juvenile, and lastly an adult.

PLANTS

A typical plant has three major sections; roots, stems, and leaves. The *roots* lie underground where they absorb water and minerals needed by the plant. These water and minerals are carried up to the leaves through special tubes in the *stem* or *trunk*. The *leaves* use the water from the roots and absorb carbon dioxide from the air. The green color in *leaves* is due to *chlorophyll*. Chlorophyll absorbs sunlight to produce a special chemical that releases energy to enable the plant to produce sugar to nourish the rest of the plant. This food-making process is called *photosynthesis*.

FLOWERING SEED-BEARING PLANTS VERSUS NONFLOWERING SEED-BEARING PLANTS

Flowering and nonflowering seed-bearing plants also have different life cycles. Flowering and nonflowering seed-bearing plants both start out as a seed, grow into a seedling or small plant, and mature into an adult that will produce its own seeds after being pollinated. Flowering plants produce flowers to hold their seeds, while nonflowering plants that produce seeds often use structures like cones to hold their seeds.

FLOWERS

Flowers are the structures which many plants reproduce. A typical flower has both male and female parts. The male *stamens* consist of a stalk called a *filament* with a swollen *anther* at the tip which produces the *pollen*. The female parts consist of an *ovary* which produces the seeds and a tube called a *pistil* through which the pollen enters to fertilize the seeds. Showy colorful *petals* surround the male and female parts. Below the petals are smaller *sepals* that are usually green.

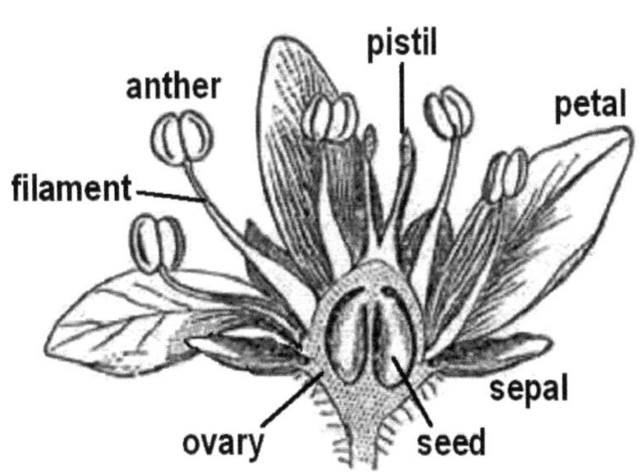

Food Manufacturing of Green Plants

Green plants use energy from sunlight and carbon dioxide from the air to make sugars and energy-carrying molecules by *photosynthesis*. This word means "to put together with light." In this process plants give off oxygen as a waste product. This oxygen is then breathed in and used by animals.

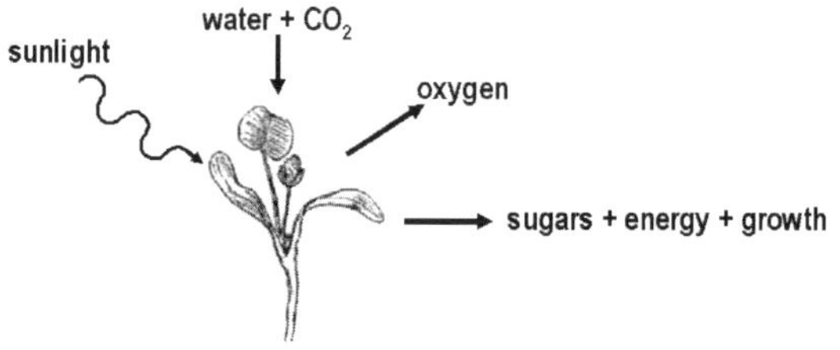

Pollination

Pollen can be carried to the female parts of other plants by wind or water. About 10% of pollination occurs this way. But most plants (80%) depend on animals for cross pollination. Many flowers produce fragrant smells and sweet nectar to attract bees, hummingbirds, other insects, and even certain kinds of bats. These animals feed on the nectar and pick up pollen on their bodies. Then when they fly to another plant the pollen is transferred to the female parts where fertilization takes place.

Trees

Certain types of trees and shrubs called *conifers* produce pollen and seeds in *cones* instead of flowers. Pines, spruces, firs, and cypresses are examples of conifers. Their leaves look like pointed needles. The female cones that produce the seeds are much larger than the male cones. The conspicuous hard, woody, overlapping *bract scales* of the cones are modified leaves. Lying just above these are thin, flat *seed scales*. Each seed scale produces two *ovules*. When the ovules are fertilized by pollen from the male cones, they develop into seeds.

Tomato Plant Life Cycle

Tomato plants undergo a series of life stages, starting at the seed. The **seed** contains all of its own nutrition for the beginning stages of life. Once it is planted, it grows into a **seedling** and starts using photosynthesis to harness energy from the Sun for life and growth. When the plant is **mature**, it produces **flowers**, which then produce the tomato fruit. The **fruit** contains seeds which then go on to become the next generation for this plant. The tomato plant usually dies after one year, so the next generation comes directly from the seeds of the previous generation.

Lima Bean Life Cycle

Lima beans have a similar life cycle to that of a tomato plant. It begins as a seed, which grows roots underground. As it grows and emerges from the soil, it becomes a seedling, which eventually becomes an adult lima bean plant. Rather than flowering, it produces leaves and pods, which contain several new seeds. These seeds are known as beans, which can be replanted or used for food.

Radish Life Cycle

Radishes also begin as a seed, which germinates into a sprout. The radish grows large leaves above ground while the root underground also grows large and round. When the plant grows into an adult, it flowers, producing more seeds. The large root underground is what most people think of as a radish, and the leaves that grow above ground are known as radish greens. Both the root and the leaves can be eaten.

Frog Life Cycle

Frogs have a very distinct life cycle. Frogs start as eggs, which hatch into tadpoles. Tadpoles live and breathe completely in the water using gills and have no legs or arms. As the tadpole begins to mature, it grows legs and eventually becomes a young frog. The young frogs then emerge from the water and usually live on land and breathe air using lungs. Some frogs are still able to live and breathe underwater throughout their adult life. Frogs then reproduce by laying eggs in the water.

Lady Beetle and Butterfly Life Cycles

Lady beetles, commonly called ladybugs, and butterflies, start their lives as eggs, which then hatch into larvae, which are similar to worms. In butterflies, these larvae are called caterpillars. The larva usually spends its life eating to build up energy for the change to its next stage. The larva eventually turns into a pupa or a chrysalis, which is a far less active stage. In this change, the larva spins a web around itself, becoming a cocoon. In this stage, the body changes form and eventually, an adult butterfly or ladybug emerges. The adult forms of both of these creatures have wings and are then able to fly and eventually produce new eggs.

Cricket Life Cycle

Crickets undergo a similar change to metamorphosing insects. They start as eggs, which hatch into **nymph** crickets. These are the same as the adult form of the insect, only they are smaller and not yet capable of reproducing. As the nymph grows, it eventually becomes an adult and can then mate and lay eggs.

Relationships Between Organisms

Organisms can interact with one another in many ways. For example, **herbivores** eat plants, and **predators**, or **carnivores**, eat other animals. Organisms can also **compete** for biotic or abiotic resources in an ecosystem. In addition, organisms can rely on each other through **mutualism**, which is a relationship between at least two organisms in which both organisms benefit from each other. One organism can also rely on another through **commensalism**, which is a relationship between at least two organisms in which one organism benefits while the other is not harmed or benefitted.

Competition between Different Organisms

Animals and plants have to compete with other species for food or nutrients, water, places to live, nesting or breeding sites, sunlight in the case of plants, and other factors in the environment that may be scarce or limited. In addition, animals and plants of the same species have to compete with each other for these resources and for the opportunity to breed and reproduce. Competition may seem harmful to some plants and animals, but it actually helps some species. Competition helps control population sizes and prevents **overpopulation**. Overpopulation of a species can be dangerous since there may not be enough resources to support all of the animals of that species or animals of other species.

Changes to Ecosystems

Most ecosystems rely on **consistent patterns** and a **balance** between organisms and resources. When something changes this balance, the ecosystem may suffer. For example, consider a grassland ecosystem. Deer are grazers, animals that eat grass, and they have natural predators, such as wolves. If something happens and the predators of the deer disappear, the ecosystem may suffer. The deer would likely become overpopulated because fewer deer would be hunted by the predators. This would become a problem because as the population grows, there may not be enough grass in the area to feed all of the deer and all of the other animals that eat grass. As a result, grass may become scarce and other animals, such as insects, would lose their habitats since there would be little grass. This situation shows that even one change can hurt many members of an ecosystem.

Humans can also harm ecosystems. For example, when a new road or building is created, it takes up land that had grass, trees, bushes, or other plants growing on it. These plants provide shelter, food, and fresh oxygen for many animals. When these resources are removed, the animals must find them elsewhere. This not only harms the original ecosystem, but it can also harm the ecosystems the animals move to. The animals can cause too much competition in the new ecosystems if there are not enough resources to provide for the new animals and the animals that were already there. If this occurs, organisms from both the old and new populations could suffer.

Traits and Environments

Each organism has **traits** that affect that organism's ability to **survive**. Some of these traits are common among different species that live in similar environments. For example, many desert animals have traits that help them either survive on a small amount of water or extract water from their surroundings. A trait may also help an organism obtain food or shelter in its environment. For example, flamingos have beaks that are shaped in a way that allows flamingos to find food underwater. Furthermore, flamingos have webbed feet so they can easily live in shallow water. Woodpeckers have beaks that are shaped in a way that allows them to find food under tree bark. In addition, they have talons so they can hold onto tree limbs and build nests. These traits help both species of bird survive in their environments.

Traits for Warding Off Predators

Many organisms have traits that protect them from predators. For example, an animal's hair color or skin color may help it blend in with its surroundings and hide. Some animals have skin that can hurt or taste bad to predators, which can lead predators to avoid trying to eat that animal. Many of these traits are the result of **adaptations**, or traits that species developed over time to help them live in their environment.

Example

Which traits would make a species more successful in an aquatic environment?

a. A beak
b. Webbed feet
c. A tail
d. Opposable thumbs

Choice A suggests a beak, which could be useful in obtaining certain types of food. A trait that would make a species more successful in an aquatic environment should be specifically related to living in water. A beak would probably be more useful on land, so Choice A is incorrect.

Choice B suggests webbed feet. Webbed feet could be useful in an aquatic environment because the extra skin between the animal's toes could be helpful for swimming. Additionally, webbed feet are unlikely to be helpful in non-aquatic environments. Choice B could be the correct answer.

Choice C suggests a tail, which is common in animals that live in many habitats, not just in the water. Choice C is not the correct answer.

Choice D suggests opposable thumbs such as those found in humans and other primates. Opposable thumbs allow animals to use tools and do things with their hands, which would be more helpful on land than in the water. Choice D is incorrect.

Choice B, webbed feet, is the only trait that is specifically related to an animal's success in an aquatic environment, making it the correct answer.

Innate Behaviors

Similar to genetics, there are some behaviors that are innate, or instinctual. Many animals do not nurture their young, but instead, the newborn creatures are capable of fending for themselves. Below are some examples of innate behaviors that are not learned or taught.

- Birds migrate from North to South for the winter to protect themselves from the cold.
- Salmon swim upstream to nesting grounds.
- Some insects migrate and form cocoons to metamorphose.
- Rattlesnakes shake their rattles to warn other animals.

Learned Behaviors

Some behaviors and traits may be inherited, but many behaviors must be taught by the parents or pack to the young. Below are some examples of learned or taught behaviors.

- A wolf pack teaches the young wolves how to hunt effectively as a group.
- Some primates use sticks as tools to gather food.
- Dogs learn tricks and commands from their owners.
- Pelicans learn to hunt for fish in groups.
- Humans teach their children words and how to read.

Adaptation to Environment

Animals and plants must be able to adapt to their environment in order to thrive or survive. Individuals must be able to recognize stimuli in their surroundings and adapt quickly. For example, an individual euglena can sense light and respond by moving toward the light. Individual organisms must also be able to adapt to changes in the environment on a larger scale. For example, plants must be able to respond to the change in the length of the day to flower at the correct time. Polar bears have white fur as camouflage which helps them blend in with their icy and snowy background. This makes it easier to sneak up on the seals on which they prey. They also have thick fur and a thick layer of blubber to help keep them warm in their frigid environment.

Organisms and Environmental Changes

Sudden environmental changes can include **natural disasters**, **diseases**, and **habitat destruction**. Examples of more **gradual** changes include **climate change** or **gradual habitat loss** due to population growth, agriculture, or the harvesting of natural resources. Both sudden and gradual environmental changes have the potential to significantly disrupt the balance of an ecosystem. When organisms die due to natural disasters, disease, or environmental changes, the number of individuals in a population changes. In more sudden environmental changes, these shifts in population numbers are more dramatic. Additionally, these changes in population numbers can have a **domino effect** on the ecosystem. For example, when a predator population decreases, the prey populations increase because of the reduced risk of being hunted. However, another predator population could increase because there is now reduced **competition** for resources. Environmental changes can also affect populations by influencing the presence of certain physical traits. Because individuals with certain traits are more likely to survive specific environmental changes, those traits will become more common in a population through the process of **natural selection.**

EXAMPLE

A remote island consisting of rainforest habitats has experienced consistently rising temperatures over the course of a decade. Scientists have made several observations of changes to local populations. Which of the following observations is most likely a beneficial change to a trait that will affect subsequent generations?

a. The population of frogs has declined.
b. Old-growth trees are producing fewer leaves.
c. Birds spend less time in the canopy.
d. A small mammal species produces a thinner coat of fur.

Choice A describes a decline in the population of frogs. Rising temperatures are likely to cause certain populations to decline, particularly amphibians. However, the question asks for an example of a beneficial change to a trait that will be inherited by subsequent populations. In this case, population decline is not a change to a trait, and population decline is rarely beneficial. Choice A is not the answer.

Choice B describes trees producing fewer leaves. This answer specifies that the trees are old-growth trees, meaning they have been around for a long time. In this case, producing fewer leaves is likely to be an individual response to limited resources and environmental changes. This is unlikely to be a beneficial change because fewer leaves mean the trees cannot photosynthesize as much. In addition, this describes an immediate survival response rather than an inherited change to a trait. Choice B is probably not the answer.

Choice C describes a change in birds' behavior, who begin to spend less time in the canopy, likely to avoid the sun. Because this is a change in behavior, it is unclear whether it would be passed on to subsequent generations. Choice C is probably not the answer.

Choice D describes a change to a physical trait, specifically fur thickness in small mammal species. With rising temperatures, having thinner fur is likely to be beneficial in keeping the animal from overheating. Additionally, a physical trait is more likely to be passed on to subsequent generations than a behavioral change. Choice D is the correct answer.

Choice D is the correct answer because it describes a change to a trait that is most likely to be beneficial and to be inherited by subsequent generations.

HUMAN IMPACT ON MARINE ENVIRONMENTS

Humans can impact ecosystems directly and indirectly. For example, humans can **directly** impact an ecosystem through deforestation and overfishing, while humans can **indirectly** impact ecosystems through the burning of fossil fuels, which can contribute to climate change and pollution. Marine ecosystems are some of the most vulnerable to these impacts. For example, the ocean absorbs some of the carbon dioxide (CO_2) that goes into the atmosphere, and so as more CO_2 goes into the atmosphere due to human activity, more CO_2 goes into the ocean. This absorption has caused chemical reactions that have led the oceans to become more acidic. This **ocean acidification** poses a threat to shell-building organisms and coral. Because coral reefs provide food and habitats for a significant portion of marine life, ocean acidification poses intense danger for marine ecosystems. Human agricultural activity also contributes to ocean pollution, as **runoff** from fertilizers and other chemicals leaks into the ocean.

Overfishing and Artificial Reefs

Reliance on oceans for food has led to **overfishing**, which is when fish are caught and removed from a body of water at a higher rate than the fish can reproduce and replenish. This threatens fish populations as well as entire marine ecosystems. To increase fish populations in a certain area, humans have used **artificial reefs**, which are created by submerging materials into the water to replicate a coral reef habitat. Although artificial reefs can quickly increase the populations of fish and other marine life, they can have negative impacts, such as contributing to ocean pollution. Ironically, they can increase the fish population so much that many people will fish there and repeat the process of overfishing. Because of this, overfishing is a cyclical process that must constantly be kept in check.

Effects of Temperature, Light, Moisture, and Air on Plant Growth

Environmental factors including temperature, light, moisture, and air can all impact plant growth. **Temperature** is the most important environmental factor determining plant growth. The temperature needs vary for different plants. Tender plants will not grow in cold conditions. Plants use photosynthesis to create food. For photosynthesis to take place, plants need **light**. Without light, plants cannot produce food and will die. Water is essential for all life, including plants. **Water** is the main component of plant cells and helps keep the plant turgid. A plant without water will wilt and die. Water is required in photosynthesis and is used to transport nutrients in the plant. **Air** is required for both the production of food (photosynthesis) and the breakdown of food into energy (respiration).

Organisms and Seasonal Changes

As the seasons change, plants and animals adopt different strategies to stay alive; however, those strategies change depending on the environment the plants and animals live in. During winter, many plants, like maple trees, go dormant. This is a process that makes them lose their leaves to help save energy. Because Florida has a milder winter, however, some plants only lose some of their leaves instead of all. During winter, many animals also go dormant by hibernating because they cannot find enough food. At the same time, many other animals migrate to places like Florida to make it through the winter. For example, black bears choose to briefly hibernate even through the temperate Florida winter, while manatees migrate to Florida in winter in search of warmth.

Animal Migration

Many animals make a regular two-way, long-distance journey due to seasonal changes affecting the availability of food, weather or rainfall. Birds are especially noted for this, but other animals like bats, some butterflies, moths, and grasshoppers also migrate back and forth between northern winter and southern summer territories. Caribou and wildebeest also make spectacular migrations. The figure at right shows the 14,000-mile migration route of the Swainson's hawk, which spends its summers in western North America and winters in South America.

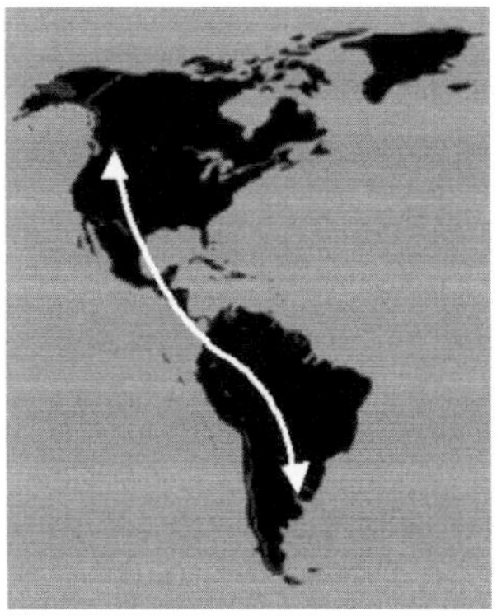

Animal Hibernation

Hibernation occurs when an animal enters a state of inactivity in which its body temperature drops, and its breathing and metabolism slow down, and it goes into a deep sleep for many days, weeks, or even months. This allows animals to survive long, cold winters when food is scarce. Bears, ground squirrels and other rodents, some bats like the one shown hibernating here, and certain kinds of snakes are known to hibernate. Some animals sleep through hot summer weather or droughts. This is called *aestivation*.

Plant Responses to Weather

Temperature, how warm or cool something is, and precipitation, water vapor in the atmosphere that falls to Earth, both influence animal and plant behavior. Plants have a different reaction than animals to changes in temperature and precipitation. In autumn, the leaves of deciduous trees change colors, and in winter, their leaves fall so the trees will use less energy and not dry out. When the temperature warms in spring, the trees regrow their leaves and create flowers. Plants that grow from bulbs, like daffodils, tulips, and hyacinths, become dormant in winter. They need to experience a period of cold temperature before they can bloom in spring along with trees.

Chapter Quiz

1. Dolphins can be found in the Atlantic Ocean off the east coast of Florida. Dolphins are warm-blooded, give live birth, feed their babies milk, and have a complex brain. According to these characteristics, dolphins are in a group with which other animals?

a. frogs, toads, salamanders
b. turtles, lizards, snakes
c. clownfish, seahorses, eels
d. humans, elephants, monkeys

2. The Florida panther is an endangered species that can be found in the Everglades.

Which of the following would NOT be a negative environmental change that would affect the population of Florida panthers in the Everglades?

a. habitat loss due to the development of highways and businesses
b. population increase of white-tailed deer, the main source of food for panthers
c. diseases caused from water pollution
d. introduction of invasive species such as the Burmese python

3. The Florida panther is the most endangered species that currently lives in the everglades of southern Florida. Which of the following has the biggest negative impact on the population of the Florida panther?

a. the increase in population of the snapping turtle
b. human interference such has the building of factories and highways
c. predators such as feral hogs and deer
d. the introduction of different plant species

4. Birds have many adaptations that allow them to survive in their environments. Which adaptation below shows a way birds adapt to the changing seasons?

a. Birds have different shaped beaks that allow them to catch worms or fish.
b. Birds' bodies are covered with feathers that help them in flight.
c. Birds lay eggs in early spring so that the babies hatch during late spring to summer.
d. Birds sometimes have webbed feet that help in swimming.

5. Which does NOT describe a way that Florida animals adapt during the winter months?

a. Sandhill cranes migrate to Florida in search of a warmer climate.
b. Manatees stay closer to each other and move to the warmer springs in Florida.
c. The metabolic rate of Florida reptiles slows down so that they use fewer calories.
d. The veiled chameleon changes colors to blend in with the trees.

6. A science class was asked to illustrate the life cycle of a common insect. One student chose the house fly. The life cycle of a house fly is pictured below.

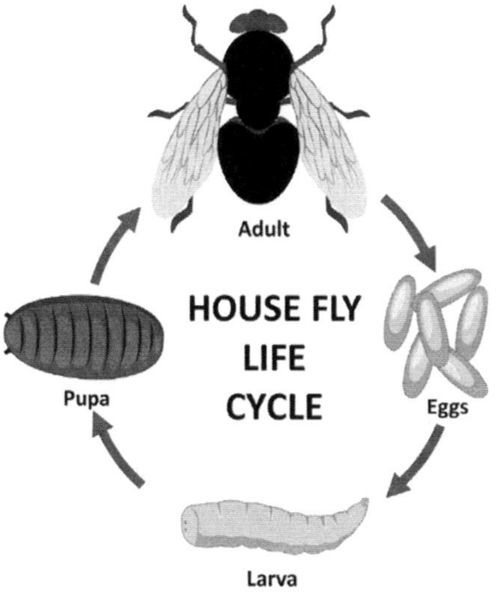

The life cycle of the house fly is most similar to which other life cycle?

a. Butterfly
b. Frog
c. Bird
d. Bat

7. A horse is an example of a(n) ________.

a. omnivore
b. carnivore
c. scavenger
d. herbivore

8. In a food chain, where does energy go after the secondary consumer dies?

a. Back to the Sun
b. To the producers
c. Into the air, becoming wind
d. To decomposers

9. A bean plant begins its life cycle as which of the following?

a. leaf
b. root
c. stem
d. seed

10. Which group of major parts and organs make up the immune system?

a. Lymphatic system, spleen, tonsils, thymus, and bone marrow
b. Brain, spinal cord, and nerve cells
c. Heart, veins, arteries, and capillaries
d. Nose, trachea, bronchial tubes, lungs, alveolus, and diaphragm

Chapter Quiz Answers and Explanations

1. D: Dolphins have the characteristics of mammals like humans, elephants, and monkeys. Frogs, toads, and salamanders are amphibians. Turtles, lizards, and snakes are reptiles. Clownfish, seahorses, and eels are fish. These are all cold-blooded animals.

2. B: A population increase of the main prey of the Florida panther would be a positive change as it would make it easier for the panther to hunt and eat. This would not be a negative environmental change. Habitat loss, diseases, and the introduction of invasive species are all negative environmental changes that have made it more difficult for the Florida panther to survive.

3. B: Humans have had the biggest negative impact on the Florida panther population in the everglades as more factories and highways have been built taking away the habitat for the Florida panther. The snapping turtle and Florida panther do not share similar habitats. Feral hogs and deer are the prey of the Florida panthers, not predators. Different plant species have little effect on the Florida panther.

4. C: Birds lay eggs so that their babies can hatch during the warmer spring season. Baby birds would have a harder time surviving in the winter because of the cold temperatures and scarce access to food. Beaks, feathers, and feet are all physical adaptations that help birds survive but are not related to the changing seasons.

5. D: Camouflage is an adaptation that chameleons use to survive, but it is not an adaptation that is specific to the changing season of winter. Migration, social patterns such as staying closer to each other, and a slowed metabolic rate are all ways that Florida animals change their patterns in the winter.

6. A: A butterfly goes through the same stages as a house fly. It starts with an egg and progresses to larva or caterpillar, then the pupa or chrysalis, and then an adult. After being born from an egg, a frog goes from a tadpole to froglet to an adult frog (B). A bird hatches from an egg and grows from a baby bird to an adult bird (C). A bat is born live, not from an egg, so its life cycle is very different from the house fly (D).

7. D: Horses eat plants but do not eat meat, so they are herbivores. Omnivores (A) eat plants and meat. Carnivores (B) eat meat but do not eat plants. Scavengers (C) consume only dead and decaying animals.

8. D: After a secondary consumer dies, such as a wolf, its body is partially consumed by decomposers, such as bacteria and fungi. Bacteria and fungi live in soil and digest body tissues of dead organisms, converting them into basic nutrients that plants need to grow. Therefore, after secondary consumers die, their energy is consumed by decomposers, who make nutrients available in the soil for producers to use. *Do not confuse nutrients in the soil with energy that producers get from the Sun to make their own food.*

9. D: Bean plants begin their lives as seeds. Then they grow roots, stems, and leaves. Therefore, the correct choice is D.

10. A: The immune system consists of the lymphatic system, spleen, tonsils, thymus, and bone marrow.

Practice Test #1

1. The life cycle of a moth and a frog are pictured below.

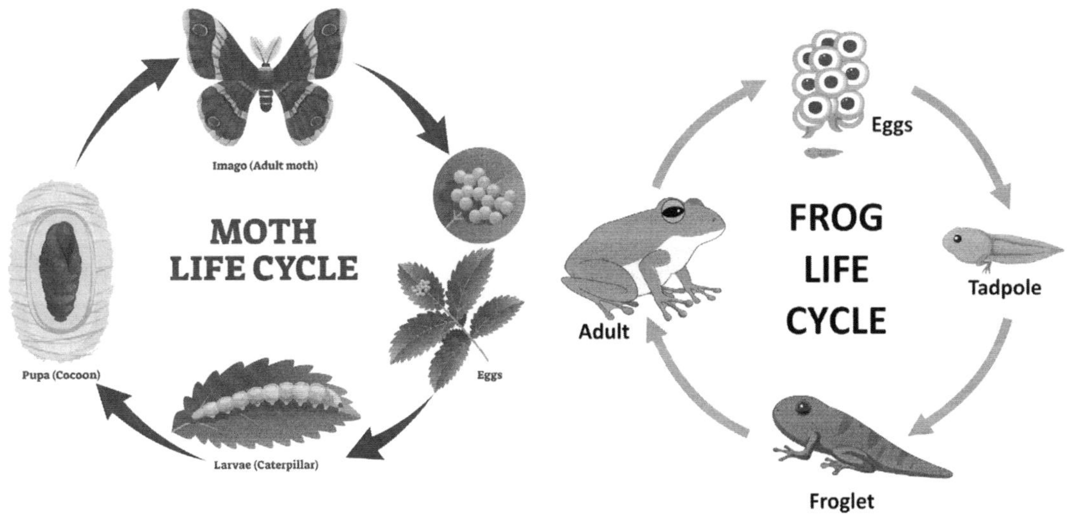

Which statement INCORRECTLY compares the life cycles of the moth and the frog?

a. The moth experiences metamorphosis during its life cycle, but the frog does not.
b. The larva stage of the moth is most like the tadpole stage of a frog.
c. The moth and the frog begin their life cycles in the same way.
d. The adult moth and the adult frog are both responsible for reproduction.

2. A grassland food chain is shown below.

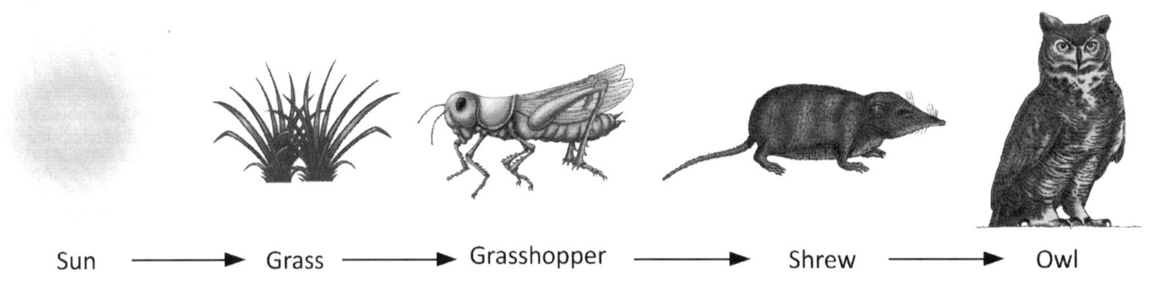

What is the producer in this food chain, and where does it receive its energy?

a. The owl is the producer, and it receives its energy from the Sun.
b. The shrew is the producer, and it receives its energy from the grasshopper.
c. The grasshopper is the producer, and it receives its energy from the grass.
d. The grass is the producer, and it receives its energy from the Sun.

3. Which correctly matches the body organ with its function?

a. Liver: helps to move blood throughout the body
b. Small intestines: absorbs nutrients from food
c. Heart: aids in breathing
d. Diaphragm: allows the body to move

4. A boy is outside in the winter and notices that he begins shivering when he gets cold. A girl is outside during the summer and begins sweating when she gets hot. Why do the children's bodies react this way?

a. The children's bodies are attempting to regulate their temperature.
b. The children's bodies are trying to fight off disease.
c. The children's bodies are reacting to the amount of sunlight or shade.
d. The children are having an allergic reaction to something in the air.

5. Lucas and Sophia compare different properties of matter. In a lab, they placed four common household items in a beaker and noted the volume and shape in the chart below.

Item	Takes Shape of Container	Fixed Volume
1	No	Yes
2	Yes	No
3	Yes	Yes
4	No	Yes

Based on their observations, which item could be lemonade?

a. Item 1
b. Item 2
c. Item 3
d. Item 4

6. Mike and Keesha are studying the night sky. They go outside right after dinner and notice that the moon is right above the tree line in the backyard. They go outside a few hours later and notice that the moon is now much higher in the sky. They want to explain to their classmates why the moon appears to move. What model should they use to explain this occurrence?

a. Use a globe and slowly turn it on its axis to demonstrate how the earth rotates, and move a small ball, representing the moon in a circle around the Earth.
b. Move a smaller ball, representing the Earth, in a circular orbit around the larger ball, representing the Sun.
c. Take a small ball, representing the moon, and move it in a circular orbit around a globe, representing the Earth.
d. Use a globe to represent the Earth and move it in a circular orbit around a small ball that represents the moon.

7. Roberto and Alexandria are writing a paragraph about the outer planets in our solar system. Their outline is shown below.

Outer Planets
Jupiter, Saturn, Uranus, Neptune
Orbit the Sun
All have rings
____

Which other fact could the students include about the outer planets?

a. Take longer to orbit the Sun than inner planets
b. Much smaller than the inner planets
c. Don't have any moons, unlike the inner planets
d. Made mostly of rock like the inner planets

8. A large container holding a mixture of similar- sized glass marbles and iron marbles arrived at the store. The clerk needs to separate the marbles before selling them at the store. What would be the best way for the clerk to separate the glass marbles and iron marbles?

a. Pour the mixture into water. The glass marbles will float to the top and the iron marbles will sink to the bottom, making them easier to separate.
b. Pour the mixture onto a flat surface. Move a strong magnet over the mixture. The iron stones will stick to the magnet separating them from the glass marbles.
c. Pour the mixture over a strainer. The glass marbles will fall through the strainer, and the iron marbles will remain in the strainer.
d. Pour the mixture into a large container that can be used to heat the contents. The glass marbles will melt leaving only the iron marbles.

9. Students were asked to write a paragraph about the similarities between comets and asteroids. Which fact about an asteroid is not a way it is similar to a comet?

a. Asteroids orbit the Sun.
b. Asteroids are smaller than planets.
c. Asteroids move through our solar system.
d. Asteroids are made of rock or metal.

10. If magnet 1 slides toward magnet 2 in the direction of the arrow, how will magnet 2 be expected to move?

a. Magnet 2 will be attracted to magnet 1 and move toward it.
b. Magnet 2 will neither attract nor repel magnet one and won't move at all.
c. Magnet 2 will first be attracted to magnet 1 and as it gets closer it will repel it.
d. Magnet 2 will repel magnet one and move away from it.

11. Students measured the weather conditions on Monday using a thermometer to measure temperature and an anemometer to measure wind speed. The readings on the weather tools are shown below.

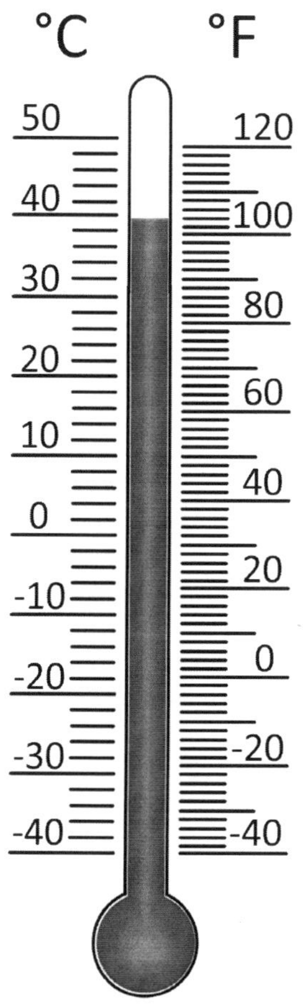

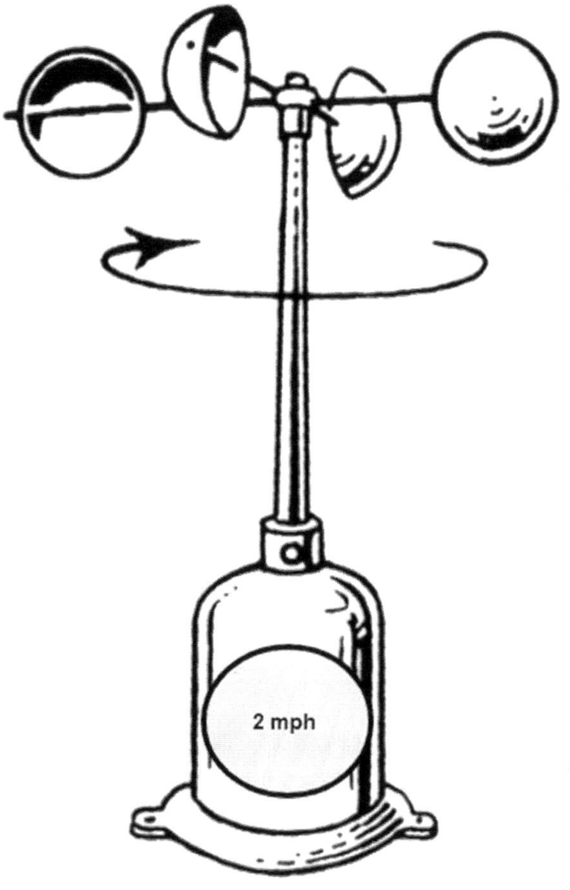

Based on these readings, which best describes the weather on Monday?

a. Windy and rainy
b. Cold and windy
c. Hot and not windy
d. Snowy and not windy

12. Why are plants considered producers?

a. They make their own food
b. They soak up water from the ground
c. Their leaves can be large or small
d. They produce pollen, which is a food source for many insects and birds

13. The image below illustrates how water droplets sometimes form on the side of a cold glass of water.

In which part of the water cycle pictured below does this process also occur?

a. Number 1
b. Number 2
c. Number 3
d. Number 4

14. The students use an electric pencil sharpener, computer, and speaker in their science classroom every day. These three common classroom items are all examples of which two types of energy?

a. Light energy and sound energy
b. Sound energy and electrical energy
c. Light energy and mechanical energy
d. Chemical energy and mechanical energy

15. Brown pelicans are common on the beaches of Florida.

Which statement correctly describes an adaptation that helps the brown pelican survive in Florida?

a. The brown pelican's long beak is a behavioral adaptation that allows the pelican to catch fish in the ocean.
b. The brown pelican laying its eggs on the sandy beach is an example of a physical adaptation.
c. The pelican's webbed feet are a physical adaptation that allows it to move quickly in ocean waters.
d. The brown pelican's northern migration pattern is a life cycle adaptation that helps it survive during the winter months.

16. Megan completed an experiment in which she tested the effects of different types of water on plants. Which of her observations CANNOT be tested?

a. The plant given sugar water grew taller than the plant given salt water.
b. The leaves on the plant given salt water turned yellow.
c. The plant given plain water does not seem as healthy as the plant given salt water.
d. The plant given salt water lost more leaves than the other plants.

17. The data below was collected by repeating the same experiment four different times. What conclusion can be drawn based on the data shown?

Bicycle Obstacle Race

Student	Trial 1	Trial 2	Trial 3	Trial 4
Kayla	57.6 s	37.6 s	37.3 s	36.2 s
Carson	64.0 s	32.6 s	31.2 s	28.4 s
Jeremy	59.2 s	31.0 s	28.8 s	27.9 s
Rachel	61.3 s	42.6 s	39.5 s	39.0 s

a. The data was accurate in all four trials
b. The data in trials 2 through 4 is probably inaccurate
c. An error occurred in trial 1 that gave inaccurate data
d. The times in trial 4 are fastest because the students were tired

18. The students were asked to sort common resources in Florida into renewable and nonrenewable groups. Below are the responses of four different students.

Student 1

Renewable	Nonrenewable
Water	Phosphate
Wind	Oil
Solar	Limestone
	Silica

Student 2

Renewable	Nonrenewable
Water	Phosphate
Wind	Limestone
Solar	Silica
Oil	

Student 3

Renewable	Nonrenewable
Limestone	Phosphate
Silica	Water
Solar	Oil
	Wind

Student 4

Renewable	Nonrenewable
Phosphate	Water
Oil	Wind
Limestone	Solar
Silica	

Which student correctly sorted the common Floridan resources?

a. student 1
b. student 2
c. student 3
d. student 4

19. Electrical cords, such as the cords of a television or the cord on a toaster, are covered with rubber or plastic. What would you expect to happen if a portion of the rubber covering were missing when you tried to plug the cord in?

a. The appliance would not work after it was plugged in
b. The person plugging the appliance in would feel an electric shock
c. The appliance being plugged in would work, but all other appliances in the home would stop working
d. The cover does not matter, all appliances would work normally

20. How are organisms, such as snakes, cacti, and coyotes, able to survive in harsh desert conditions?

a. Over thousands of years these organisms have developed adaptations to survive in arid climates
b. These organisms migrate out of the desert during the summer months, only living in the desert for a portion of the year
c. Snakes, cacti, and coyotes work together to find sources of food and water
d. Snakes, cacti, and coyotes are all aquatic species that live in ponds and rivers during the hot day

21. Lincoln explains that our galaxy is known as the Milky Way galaxy, and that all galaxies contain gas and dust. What other main part of a galaxy did Lincoln forget to mention?

a. Planets with rings
b. Six or more moons
c. Many stars
d. Several asteroids

22. The observations outlined below were made about a pot of water over a campfire. What is the most likely explanation for these observations?

The pot was half full of water.
The pot hung over the campfire for 15 minutes.
The water began boiling after 7 minutes.
A white vapor was observed over the pot.
After 15 minutes, the pot was one quarter of the way full.

a. Some of the water disappeared
b. The water changes from a gas to a liquid
c. Some of the water changed from a liquid to a gas, which was the vapor observed
d. The pot was never half full, someone measured incorrectly

23. Based on the weather forecast, what can a farmer expect to happen to his bird bath overnight?

10pm	11pm	12am	1am	2am	3am	4am	5am
34°C	25°C	11°C	2°C	-4 °C	-12 °C	-18°C	-18°C

a. Freeze
b. Evaporate
c. Melt
d. Sublime

24. What question are the students most likely testing with the experiment outlined below?

Seed type: Pansy	Seed type: Pansy	Seed type: Pansy
Water: ½ gallon daily	Water: ½ gallon daily	Water: ½ gallon daily
Soil: Bob's soil	Soil: Texas dirt	Soil: Grow Up Dirt
Daylight: 3 hours per day	Daylight: 3 hours per day	Daylight: 3 hours per day
Flower color: Blue	Flower color: Purple	Flower color: Red

a. Does the amount of water affect how tall a flower will grow?
b. Does the type of soil affect the color of a flower?
c. What color of flower do bees prefer?
d. Is three hours of daylight enough for flowers to grow?

25. Lauren completed a scientific investigation in which she tested the buoyancy of various objects. Lauren recorded the steps to her experiment carefully and precisely. If she gave those steps to her friend, what would be the expected result?

a. At the end of the investigation, Lauren's friend should have created a new experiment.
b. Lauren's friend will not be able to complete the investigation because Lauren did not share her results.
c. Lauren's friend will need to use different materials for the investigation to be considered valuable.
d. At the end of the investigation, Lauren's friend should have completed the procedures and gathered similar evidence.

Answer Key and Explanations for Test #1

1. A: SC.4. L.16.4

Although the moth experiences a more obvious body change than the frog during its lifecycle, both organisms experience metamorphosis, a body change. The frog grows legs and absorbs its tail and the moth changes from a worm-like organism to a flying creature. Both the moth and the frog begin their life cycle as eggs and the larva stage of a moth is similar to the tadpole stage of a frog. The adult moth and the adult frog both reproduce by laying eggs.

2. D: SC.4. L.17.3

The grass is the producer because it makes its own food and does not rely on another organism for its nutrients. The grass receives energy from the Sun that allows it to make its own food. The grasshopper, shrew, and owl are examples of consumers because they need other organisms for food.

3. B: SC.5.L.14.1

The small intestine is where nutrients are absorbed. The liver breaks down food, the heart pumps blood, and the diaphragm allows for air to enter and exit the lungs.

4. A: SC.5.L.14.1

The human body works best within a certain temperature range, around 98.6˚F. When the body gets too cold or too hot it cannot function properly. The boy who is outside in the winter is cold. His body temperature is dropping below 98.6˚F. His muscles start to contract causing him to shiver in order to generate heat. The girl is outside in the summer, and begins sweating to reduce her body temperature from rising too far above 98.6°F. In both cases, the children's bodies are trying to keep the temperature close to 98.6˚F.

5. C: SC.5.P.8.1

Item 3 could be lemonade because lemonade is a liquid and liquids take the shape of their container and have a fixed volume. Item 1 and item 4 are solids because they do not take the shape of their container, but they do have a fixed volume. Item 2 is a gas because it does take the shape of its container, but it does not have a fixed volume.

6. A: SC.4.E.5.4

Spinning a globe on its axis while moving the moon in an orbit around Earth would model that the moon appears to be moving in the sky at night because the Earth is rotating on its axis. Moving the Earth in an orbit around the Sun would explain the seasonal changes on Earth. Modeling that the moon orbits the Earth does not explain why the moon appears to move across the sky. The Earth does not orbit the moon.

7. A: SC.5.E.5.2

The outer planets take longer to orbit the Sun than the inner planets. Their orbit is longer because they are farther away from the Sun. The outer planets are larger than the inner planets; they all have moons, and they are made of gas or ice.

8. B: SC.5.P.8.3

Since the iron marbles are magnetic and the glass marbles are not magnetic, the best way to separate this mixture would be using a magnet. Glass and iron both sink in water, so pouring the mixture into water would not be beneficial. Since the marbles are similar in size, pouring the mixture over a strainer would not aid in the separation process. Heating is not a good way to sort this mixture because it will ruin the marbles. The iron marbles will likely melt before the glass marbles, but heating would ruin both marbles and is not a good way to sort this type of mixture.

9. D: SC.5.E.5.3

Asteroids are made of rock or metal, but comets are made of frozen rock and ice and dust. Both asteroids and comets revolve around the Sun, are smaller in size than planets, and travel through our solar system.

10. D: SC.4.P.8.4

Since the same pole on both magnets are facing each other, they will repel each other and magnet 2 will slide away from magnet one. If magnet 1 was flipped around the north pole it would be attracted to the south pole, and magnet 2 would move toward magnet 1. Magnets are either attracted or repelled, and they do not go from attracting to repelling as distance is decreased.

11. C: SC.5.E.7.3

The temperature on the thermometer reads over 100 degrees Fahrenheit which means it is a hot day. The anemometer shows the wind only blowing 2 miles per hour which means it is not windy. Neither of these tools measure the rain. The temperature indicates that it is hot, way too warm for snow.

12. A: SC.5.L.14.2

Plants are considered producers because they are able to absorb light energy from the Sun and convert it into food through the process of photosynthesis. In other words, plants are producers because they produce their own food from sunlight.

13. B: SC.5.E.7.1

The water droplets form on the glass of ice water as the water vapor in the air is cooled which is called condensation. Condensation is also illustrated at number 2 on the water cycle diagram as the water vapor in the air is cooler and forms water droplets in the clouds. Number one in the water cycle diagram illustrates evaporation, number 3 illustrates precipitation, and number 4 illustrates runoff.

14. B: SC.5.P.10.1

The electric pencil sharpener, computer, and speaker are all examples of both sound energy since they all produce noise and electrical energy since they all must be plugged into electrical sources for power. Although the computer is an example of light energy, the pencil sharpener and speaker are not. The pencil sharpener is an example of mechanical energy, but the other two items are not. Since the items use electrical energy for power, they are not examples of chemical energy.

15. C: SC.5.L.17.1

The brown pelican's webbed feet are like paddles in the water and help the bird to swim quickly in the ocean. This is an example of a physical adaptation because it describes a body part that helps the animal to survive in its environment. The pelican's beak is also an example of a physical adaptation, not a behavior adaptation. Laying eggs in a specific location is an example of a life cycle adaptation, and migration is an example of a behavior adaptation.

16. C: SC.5.N.2.1

The plain water plant seeming less healthy is a personal interpretation and not based on observable data that can be tested. The height of the plant, the color of the plant, and the number of leaves on the plant can all be observed and tested again.

17. C: SC.5.N.1.3

The data is relatively consistent with the exception of trial 1. When an experiment is repeated using the same process multiple times, the data from each trial should be very similar or the same. The results of trial 1 indicate that an error may have occurred in the procedure yielding inaccurate results.

18. A: SC.4.E.6.3

Water, wind, and solar resources are all renewable because they can continue to be replaced through the natural processes of the Earth. Phosphate, oil, limestone, and silica are all nonrenewable resources because they take a long time to be created and cannot be replaced as fast as they are being used.

19. B: SC.5.P.11.2

The purpose of the rubber coating on the outside of electrical cords is to contain the electric current in the metal wire. When part of the rubber coating is missing, the electric current can leave the wire and cause an electric shock to the person plugging in the wire.

20. A: SC.5.L.17.1

Many organisms, especially organisms that live in harsh conditions such as deserts or frozen icy areas, have developed specific adaptations that allow them to survive. For example, cacti are able to expand to store large amounts of water, coyotes absorb some water from their food, and snakes can escape the heat by hiding within rocks.

21. C: SC.5.E.5.1

Galaxies are made up of gas, dust, and a multitude of stars and all the celestial bodies that orbit those stars. Although galaxies can have planets with rings, six or more moons, and several asteroids, these elements are not required in a galaxy.

22. C: SC.5.P.9.1

Water boils at 100°C. As the pot of water heats up over the campfire, it begins to boil causing the liquid water to turn into water vapor, a gas. The vapor the campers observed over the boiling pot of water was water vapor. As the water continues to boil, more of the liquid turns into gas resulting in a decrease in the volume of water in the pot.

23. A: SC.5.P.9.1

The weather forecast shows that a cold front will be arriving in the area causing the temperature to drop from 34°C to -18°C. The freezing point of water is 0°C, which means that the water in the birdbath will freeze overnight after the cold front arrives.

24. B: SC.5.N.1.1

In order to determine the question being tested, you must look at the data given. Answer choice A asks about how tall a flower will grow, but the height of the flowers is not given, so this cannot be what was tested. Answer choice C asks about bees, which are also not referenced anywhere in the experiment. Answer choice D asks about the amount of daylight required for the flowers to grow. All three flowers were given the same amount of daylight- three hours, so this cannot be what is tested. The only change between each of the tests is the type of dirt used, which affected the flower color.

25. D: SC.5.N.2.2

Since Lauren's friend was given clear steps, the investigation should be able to be replicated and result in similar evidence. If the friend follows the steps, the results would be a similar experiment, not a new one. Lauren's friend can complete the investigation because she was given clear steps. The results are not needed to replicate the investigation. The same materials must be used, or the second experiment does not add to the validity of the first.

Practice Test #2

1. A specific part of a plant is indicated in the image below.

Which is NOT a function of this part of a plant?

a. To move water from the roots to other parts of the plant
b. To provide stability for the plant
c. To produce food for the plant
d. To transport nutrients throughout the plant

2. The digestive system is responsible for breaking down food in the body. Which correctly illustrates the order food is processed through the organs of the digestive system?

a. Mouth to stomach to intestines to pancreas
b. Mouth to esophagus to intestines to liver
c. Mouth to esophagus to stomach to intestines
d. Mouth to liver to intestines to stomach

3. During science class, students worked to classify different objects into four different groups based on their observable properties. The chart they created is below.

Observable Property	Group 1	Group 2	Group 3	Group 4
Color	Orange	Orange	Yellow	Yellow
Texture	Sticky	Bumpy	Fuzzy	Pokey
Magnetic	Yes	No	No	No
Shape	Round	Round	Flat	Flat

Students were asked to find one more object that would belong in group 2. Which object would be BEST for the students to choose?

a. Lollipop
b. Soccer Ball
c. Playdough
d. Basketball

4. Which is NOT an example of energy causing a change?

a. The dew on the grass in the morning is gone by midafternoon.
b. The wind moves the sailboat across the lake, but no one is on board.
c. The golf ball sits on the tee on the green at the driving range.
d. The ocean tide drags small shells back into the ocean.

5. A student pushes a box around the classroom collecting extra books from classmates' desks. As more books are added to the box, it becomes harder to push. Which of the following would make it easier to move the box?

a. Balance the force by adding a few more books to the box.
b. Decrease the force having one student pull the box while another student pushes the box in the opposite direction.
c. Increase the force by having another student help to push the box in the same direction.
d. Increase the force by increasing the speed at which the box is moving.

6. Vincent and Elizabeth are investigating forces using a kickball. Vincent kicks the ball straight into the air and then the ball falls back down onto the ground. What forces are causing the ball to move up and then down?

a. Friction and a push
b. Friction and gravity
c. A push and gravity
d. Magnetism and friction

7. A student is building a model of the Solar System using produce from the local supermarket. What order should she put the objects in to correctly represent the Solar System?

Object in Solar System	Model	Object in Solar System	Model
Mars	Raspberry	Uranus	tomato
Saturn	Grapefruit	Mercury	raisin
The Sun	Watermelon	Venus	grape
Jupiter	Lettuce	Asteroid Belt	sunflower seeds
Earth	Cherry	Neptune	orange

a. Watermelon-raisin-grape-cherry-raspberry-tomato-orange-lettuce-grapefruit-seeds
b. Watermelon-raisin-grape-cherry-raspberry-seeds-lettuce-grapefruit-tomato-orange
c. Watermelon-lettuce-grapefruit-tomato-orange-cherry-grape-raspberry-raisin-seeds
d. Watermelon-grape-raisin-cherry-seeds-raspberry-lettuce-grapefruti-orange-tomato

8. Students are experimenting with the physical properties of a few common minerals. The students are asked to complete the following tasks for each mineral.

1. Use the floor wheel to match the mineral with the correct color name.
2. Shine a flashlight directly onto the mineral and describe how it reflects the light from the flashlight.
3. See if you can scratch the mineral with your fingernail.
4. Rub the mineral on the white tile and record what it leaves behind.
5. Try to break the mineral with a hammer and record the results.

Steps 2 and 4 are testing which physical property of the mineral?

a. Luster and hardness
b. Cleavage and streak
c. Cleavage and color
d. Luster and streak

9. Students conduct an experiment on the school's track to determine how different types of activity affect heart rate. The experiment is outlined below.

HEART RATE EXPERIMENT

- Student One walks around the track one time and then his heart rate is recorded after he crosses the finish line.
- Student One jogs around the track one time, and then his heart rate is recorded after he crosses the finish line.
- Student One runs around the track one time, and then his heart rate is recorded after he crosses the finish line.

Student	Activity	Heart Rate
One	walk	110 beats per minute
One	jog	185 beats per minute
One	run	220 beats per minute

Which of the following changes would best make their experiment more reliable?

a. Have Student One complete the activities somewhere else besides the track.
b. Ask Student One to wear different types of shoes during each different activity.
c. Repeat the experiment with a few more students to see what patterns emerge.
d. Conduct the experiment on a rainy day, sunny day, and cloudy day.

10. A scientist wrote the following observations about a rock formation he had been studying for many years.

Over time the large rock formation began to change as the wind and the river that flowed through the area broke down pieces of the rock. The broken rock was carried away with the running river. The appearance of the rock was changed over a period of ten years.

What statement is true about the scientist's observations?

a. The scientist is only describing weathering because the observations only discuss how the rock is broken down over time.
b. The scientist is only describing erosion because the observations only describe wind and water as the way the rock was broken down.
c. The scientist is describing both weathering and erosion because the observations describe the rock breaking down and being moved to a new location.
d. The scientist is describing weathering and cementation because the observations describe the change in the rock and the formation of a new rock.

11. Students were asked to write a sentence explaining where most of the water that is evaporated in our world comes from. Which student wrote the correct explanation?

a. Most of the evaporated water in the world comes from the oceans because the oceans are the largest source of water in our world.
b. Lakes are the largest source for water evaporation because it is fresh water.
c. Water is mostly evaporated from creeks because the moving water in creeks allows evaporation to happen more quickly.
d. Ponds are responsible for most of the evaporation in our world because the creatures that live in the pond add warmth, which speeds up evaporation.

12. Students conduct two experiments to investigate the electrical charges

Experiment 1: A balloon is charged by rubbing it on a piece of wool cloth. The balloon is placed over a Styrofoam plate and the Styrofoam plate sticks to the balloon.

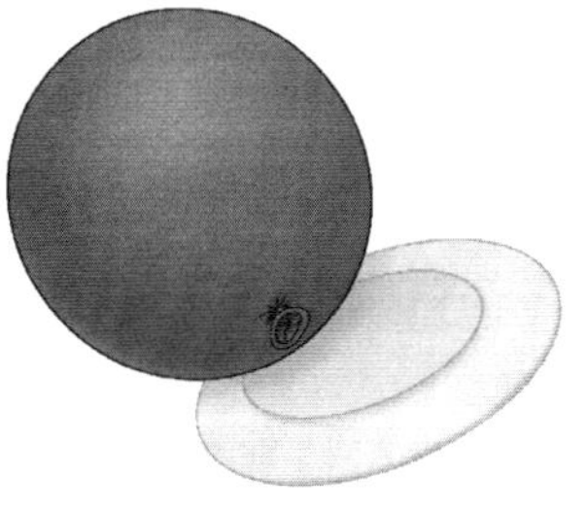

Experiment 2: Both balloons are charged by rubbing them on a piece of wool cloth. The balloon is placed next to the other balloon hanging from a string and the balloon on the string moves away from the other balloon.

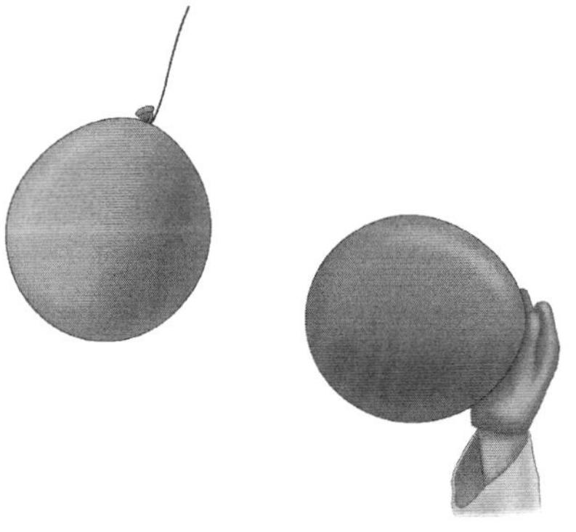

Which statement explains the results of the experiments?

a. In experiment 1, the Styrofoam has a similar charge as the balloon, so it is attracted to the balloon. In experiment 2, the balloons have different charges and repel each other.
b. In experiment 1, the Styrofoam is uncharged, and the balloon is charged so the plate is attracted to the balloon. In experiment 2, the balloons have a similar charge and repel each other.
c. In experiment 1, the Styrofoam is more charged than the balloon, so it moves closer to the balloon. In experiment 2, the balloon on the string is repelled because of wind resistance.
d. In experiment 1, the balloon does not have a charge since it was rubbed onto the wool cloth, so it is attracted to the Styrofoam plate, which is also uncharged. In experiment 2, the balloons have the same charges and repel each other.

13. The oceans are where much of the Earth's water is collected as a part of the water cycle. The water gets heated by the Sun and evaporates out of the oceans. What term describes the process that allows the oceans to collect more water again?

a. Condensation
b. Precipitation
c. Transportation
d. Transpiration

14. For the results of a scientific experiment to be considered valid and taken seriously, what must happen?

a. The results should be similar to that of other scientists.
b. The results must be the same as the hypothesis and predictions previously stated.
c. There must be numerous diagrams and charts supporting the results.
d. The results must be backed up with observable evidence.

15. One student hypothesizes that adding sports drink powder to water will help the flowers on a plant grow brighter than if it was just watered with regular water. The student places two identical daisy plants in pots on his front porch. Each day he waters one daisy with plain water and the other daisy with water mixed with sports drink powder. At the end of the week, he plans to see if the daisy watered with the sports drink powder mix has a brighter color than the other daisy. In this experiment, which part represents the control group?

a. The daisy watered with the sports drink powder mix.
b. The pots the daisies are in.
c. The daisy watered with plain water.
d. The amount of liquid used to water the daisy.

16. In ancient times humans would rub two sticks together very quickly to try to start a fire. Why would this work?

a. Rubbing wooden items together often creates an electrical spark and could lead to fire.
b. When two items are rubbed together quickly, heat is produced and could lead to fire.
c. Rubbing items together decreases air temperature and leads to the sticks catching fire.
d. When wood is rubbed together it begins to break apart and the pieces of wood can catch fire.

17. The meteorologist reported that a low-pressure system would be moving through Florida on Monday. The meteorologist showed the thermometer below to model the high temperature for Monday.

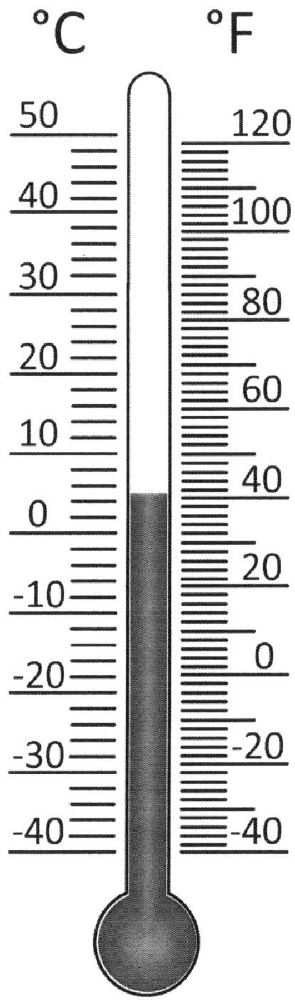

According to the meteorologist's weather forecast, which would be the most appropriate attire for a student to wear to school on Monday?

a. T-shirt and sandals
b. Rain boots and shorts
c. Raincoat and warm gloves
d. Tennis shoes and a sleeveless shirt

18. A tropical flower is planted in a local garden. The garden is watered 2 to 3 times per week during all seasons. After only a few months the tropical plant begins to droop and turn brown. How did environmental change most likely affect the tropical plant?

a. Being watered 2 to 3 times per week was not enough to sustain a tropical plant.
b. The new environment was too hot and burned the plant.
c. Insects attacked the plant causing it to wilt.
d. The new soil lacked the nutrients necessary to maintain the plant's health.

19. Polar bears, seals and walrus' are all arctic animals that have a thick layer of blubber or fat beneath their skin. What purpose does this layer of blubber serve?

a. Protects them from predators
b. Helps to preserve body heat
c. Aids in finding food
d. Prevents them from drowning in water

20. Why do some cacti have folds in their outer skin?

a. The folds can expand, allowing the cacti to absorb and store water when it rains.
b. The folds help protect the cacti from predators.
c. The folds allow them to absorb nutrients from the air.
d. The folds provide support, allowing the cacti to grow tall.

21. Algae are part of many food chains. How do algae produce energy?

algae fish seal shark

a. They hunt fish for food.
b. Algae undergo photosynthesis.
c. They decompose dead or dying organisms.
d. They consume fossil fuel from beneath Earth's surface.

22. Harrison is investigating the strength of magnets. He is going to test various sizes and shapes of magnets to see which can attract a small paper clip at the greatest distance. Harrison's teacher told him to make sure to record the steps to his experiment very carefully. Why would Harrison's teacher give this advice?

a. The steps must be recorded so that the teacher will know he actually completed the investigation.
b. The steps must be recorded so that no one will complete the exact same investigation.
c. If clear steps are recorded properly, the investigation can be replicated more easily.
d. Recording the steps in the experiment will make the investigation less reliable.

23. Why is it more difficult to push a shopping cart full of groceries than an empty shopping cart?

a. The full cart has less mass than the empty cart.
b. The full cart has a greater mass than the empty cart.
c. The full cart has less friction than the empty cart.
d. The empty cart is not pulled down by gravity.

24. Which statement describes how Earth's relationship to the Sun allows the polar ice caps to remain frozen?

a. The equator receives the most direct sunlight while the poles receive the least amount of sunlight.
b. The Moon reflects the Sun's light away from the North and South Pole preventing them from heating up.
c. Wind currents constantly move air warmed by the Sun away from the North and South Pole and toward the equator.
d. The Sun does not shine on the North or South Pole so they never warm up.

25. An ice cube tray is filled with water. The tray is placed in a freezer for 12 hours. The water freezes forming ice. The tray is removed from the freezer and left on a counter for 12 hours. What changes as the water becomes ice and then melts back into water?

a. The amount of energy in the water.
b. The amount of water in the ice cube tray.
c. The number of water molecules.
d. The mass of the water molecules.

Answer Key and Explanations for Test #2

1. C: SC.3.L.14.1

The image indicates the stem of the plant which provides stability for the plant and transports water and nutrients throughout the plant. Food is produced in the leaves and is not a function of the stem.

2. C: SC.5.L.14.1

When digesting food, the food travels from the mouth through the esophagus to the stomach and through the small and large intestines. The liver and pancreas make juices that help to break down food.

3. D: SC.4.P.8.1

A basketball would belong best in group 2 since it is usually orange in color, it has a bumpy texture, it is not magnetic, and it is round in shape. A lollipop would not belong because it does not have a bumpy texture. A soccer ball would not belong because it is not typically orange or bumpy. Playdough would not belong in group 2 because it does not have a bumpy texture and isn't always round.

4. C: SC.5.P.10.2

The golf ball simply sits on the tee without any interference causing motion or change so it is not an example of energy causing change. The energy from the sun causes a change by heating the dew on the morning grass and causing it to evaporate. The wind creates the energy needed to move the sailboat across the lake. The ocean tides provide the energy that causes the shells to move back into the ocean.

5. C: SC.5.P.13.2

The box would move more easily with an increased force. The force can be increased by adding another student as an additional source of force to push the box in the same direction. The force cannot be increased by increasing the speed. Balancing the forces would cause the box to not move at all, and decreasing the force would make it harder to move the box.

6. C: SC.5.P.13.1

Vincent pushes the ball causing it to move up in the air, and gravity pulls the ball back down to the ground. This example does not illustrate friction slowing down the kickball. Kickballs are not magnetic, and magnetism is not responsible for the movement of the ball.

7. B: SC.5.E.5.3

This question is really asking you to determine the correct order of the major bodies in the Solar System. The correct order is: Sun (watermelon), Mercury (raisin), Venus (grape), Earth (cherry), Mars (raspberry), asteroid belt (seeds), Jupiter (lettuce), Saturn (grapefruit), Uranus (tomato), Neptune (orange).

8. D: SC.4.E.6.2

Shining a light on the mineral and describing how it reflects the light is testing the luster of the mineral. Rubbing the mineral on a white tile and seeing what color rubs off on the tile is observing the streak. Hardness is tested in step 3. Cleavage would be observed in step 5. Color is observed in step 1.

9. C: SC.5.N.1.1

Repeating the experiment with other students will allow more data to be gathered that will prove that the more effort the activity requires, the higher your heart rate will be. Changing the location of the activities will have little to no effect on the results. Having the student wear different shoes or conducting the experiment in different weather conditions adds another variable to the experiment and will make the results less reliable.

10. C: SC.4.E.6.4

The scientist describes weathering when he notes that the wind and the river broke down pieces of the rock formation, and the scientist describes erosion when he describes the rock pieces being transported by the river. Erosion is not dependent on wind and water alone, and cementation is not described in the observations.

11. A: SC.5.E.7.2

Since the oceans are the largest source of water in our world, most evaporation occurs from the ocean. Fresh water does evaporate slightly faster than salt water, but lakes do not provide nearly the amount of water to be evaporated as the oceans do. Running water in creeks and higher temperatures in ponds will also aid in evaporation, but the amount of water in the sources is much smaller than the amount of water in oceans.

12. B: SC.5.P.10.3

Since the Styrofoam was uncharged and the balloon was charged, they are attracted to each other. Since the balloons in experiment 2 are both charged, they repel each other. Objects with opposite charges will be attracted to each other, but objects with similar charges will repel each other. The Styrofoam plate does not have an electrical charge in this experiment. The balloon on the string is repelled by the similarly charged balloon, not by wind. Rubbing the balloon on the wool cloth creates a charged balloon.

13. B: SC.5.E.7.1

Precipitation is responsible for replenishing the water that gets evaporated out of the ocean, and it can come in the form of rain, snow, sleet, or hail. Condensation does not refill the oceans of the Earth, but it is the process in which water vapor is cooled and turned back into small drops of water. Transportation describes movement from one place to the next. Transpiration deals with water evaporating from plant leaves.

14. D: SC.5.N.2.1

For the results of a scientific experiment to be considered valid, there must be observable evidence to back up those results. The observable evidence can be shown through diagrams and charts, but this is not the only way to provide evidence. The results of science do not always back up what has been previously agreed on by other scientists. The hypothesis and predictions are just guesses and do not have to be correct for the results to be valid.

15. C: SC.5.N.1.4

The daisy watered with plain water represents the control group because the water is what is regularly used to water the plant. The daisy watered with the sports drink powder and water is the variable in the experiment. The pot and the amount of liquid used do not affect the hypothesis of the experiment.

16. B: SC.3.P.11.2

When the sticks, or other items, are rubbed together quickly, friction between the two objects creates heat. Two wooden sticks would not produce anything related to electricity. Rubbing items together creates friction and actually increases the temperature. The breaking apart of the sticks would not lead to fire.

17. C: SC.5.E.7.3

A low pressure system indicates precipitation, and the temperature of 40 degrees Fahrenheit is cold; therefore, a raincoat and warm gloves would be appropriate attire to wear to school. A t-shirt and sandals or tennis shoes and a sleeveless shirt would be more appropriate on a warm day when a high-pressure system is moving through Florida, so neither choice A nor choice D is correct. Rain boots would be appropriate for this day, but pants should be worn with the temperature given, so choice B is incorrect.

18. A: SC.5.L.15.1

Tropical environments typically receive rain 5 to 6 times per week, even if it is only a brief afternoon shower. In its new environment the tropical plant is not receiving enough water to survive.

19. B: SC.5.L.17.1

Polar bears, seals, and walrus' all live in arctic climates where it is very cold all year round. The thick layer of blubber that these animals have below the surface of their skin helps them preserve body heat keeping them warm in the frigid environment.

20. A: SC.5.L.17.1

Cacti live in a desert environment where water is scarce. When it rains, cacti must be able to absorb and store as much water as possible so that they have water available during the dry periods. The folds on the outside of a cactus allow it to expand and fill with water. After a heavy rain, cacti will appear round and plump because the folds are full of water.

21. B: SC.5.L.14.2

Algae are a type of plant that grows in water. Because algae are plants they are able to capture light from the Sun and transform it into energy during the process of photosynthesis.

22. C: SC.5.N.2.2

When scientific investigations are carried out, the evidence should be able to be replicated by anyone else who completed the same investigation. Carefully recording the steps to the investigation will allow this to happen. The purpose of recording the steps is not to prove the experiment took place, but to make it possible to replicate exactly. Scientific investigations should be able to be easily replicated by others which makes the investigation more reliable, not less.

23. B: SC.5.P.13.3

The empty shopping cart does not weigh very much and is easy to push. As groceries are added to the empty cart, the cart gains mass. By the time the shopping cart is full, it has more mass than it began with and requires more force to push it.

24. A: SC.5.E.7.6

The equator receives the most direct sunlight while the North and South Pole receive the least amount of direct sunlight. In addition, the atmosphere helps to reflect some of the Sun's heat energy away from the poles. Finally, the reflectivity of the ice helps to deflect some of the heat away from the polar ice caps.

25. A: SC.5.P.9.1

When water changes from a liquid to a solid the amount of thermal energy is decreasing. The molecules move closer together, which creates the solid crystal structure of the ice. As the ice melts back into a liquid, thermal energy level increases, causing the molecules to spread out again.

Practice Test #3

1. The live oak tree can be found all over the state of Florida.

The trunk and bark of the live oak tree has a similar function to which part of another common organism found in Florida?

a. The gills of a sailfish
b. The exoskeleton of an apple snail
c. The feathers of a blue heron
d. The claws of the Florida black bear

2. The science teacher showed a video of a baseball in motion. What change must occur to an object for it to be in motion?

a. A mass change must occur for an object to be in motion.
b. A position change must occur for an object to be in motion.
c. A frictional change must occur for an object to be in motion.
d. A gravitational change must occur for an object to be in motion.

3. Students were asked to write about a chemical change that occurred due to a temperature change. Which student wrote the correct response?

a. Student 1: Dew formed on the morning grass when the water vapor in the air was heated by the sun.
b. Student 2: The copper bowl was hammered with a small, heated mallet to add texture and design to the bowl.
c. Student 3: The metal nails on the deck began to rust after several months of exposure to cold snow.
d. Student 4: The log turned to ash when it was burned in the fireplace.

4. Which of the following is NOT true about all galaxies?

a. Many stars make up a galaxy.
b. Celestial objects that orbit stars are also part of galaxies.
c. Planets are not a part of galaxies.
d. Galaxies contain dust particles and gases.

5. Many invertebrates such as crabs and shrimp can be found in the Atlantic Ocean along the east coast of Florida. Which other organism is an invertebrate that can be found in the Atlantic Ocean?

a. Sea otter
b. Lobster
c. Whale
d. Seal

6. Stella wants to create a model to illustrate how condensation works as part of the water cycle. Which of the following models would work best to illustrate this concept?

a. Stella could put a pot of water on a hot plate to illustrate how when water is heated, it turns to water vapor.
b. Stella could show the students the water particles that are formed on the outside of a glass of ice to illustrate how water vapor is cooled.
c. Stella could use an eye dropper to drop tiny drops of water into a tray to show how the water combines quickly.
d. Stella could put a heat lamp over a tank of water to show how water vapor is formed.

7. Isabella and Alexander are working together to write a song that can be played on their guitars. They want to change the sound of the song by increasing the pitch. How can the guitar players make this happen?

a. They can pluck the strings more slowly, so there is more time between vibrations.
b. They can tighten the guitar strings, so the strings vibrate faster.
c. They can loosen the guitar strings, so the strings vibrate slower.
d. They can adapt the guitar, so that longer strings can be used.

8. The scientific data Albert produced in his experiment was not considered valid. What might be the reason for this conclusion?

a. He did not use consistent measuring tools such a scale or measuring tape.
b. He did not start with a question.
c. He did not make a hypothesis before stating the experiment.
d. He completed the experiment more than once.

9. The hibiscus is a common plant found in tropical areas of Florida.

Which correctly describes the main purpose of flowers and leaves on plants?

a. The flowers move the nutrients through the plant. The leaves add stability.
b. The flowers help the plant reproduce. The leaves are where food is made.
c. The flowers absorb water and nutrients. The leaves help the plant reproduce.
d. The flowers attract the sun. The leaves gather water.

10. The human body sends signals to initiate movement or to warn of dangers. Which pair of organs below work closely together to send these signals?

a. Brain and spinal cord
b. Lungs and stomach
c. Heart and bladder
d. Eyes and pancreas

11. After completing an experiment on mixing different substances and observing the outcome, the students were asked to turn and tell their partner an observation they made during the experiment. Which statement below is an observation?

a. The baking soda and vinegar mixture was more exciting than the water and oil mixture.
b. The oil and water mixture was harder to observe than the baking soda and vinegar mixture.
c. When the baking soda was added to the vinegar, the mixture foamed and rose in the container.
d. The oil separated from the water more quickly than expected.

12. Students used a hygrometer to determine the humidity present on several spring days in a coastal area of Florida. They compared their results with the weather reports from a more inland location in Florida. The comparison is shown below.

DAY	HUMIDITY IN INLAND AREA	HUMIDITY IN COASTAL AREA
Monday	57%	75%
Tuesday	63%	82%
Wednesday	52%	79%

Which statement below is NOT true based on the observations in the chart?

a. The highest humidity in both areas occurred on Tuesday.
b. The humidity in the coastal area was greater than the humidity in the inland area.
c. The lowest humidity for both areas occurred on Monday.
d. The humidity during the three days was always the lowest in the inland areas.

13. Students are completing a lab with some common minerals found on the Earth. They are asked to describe how shiny or dull each mineral is and the color left behind when the mineral is rubbed on a white piece of cardboard. What properties of minerals are the students exploring?

a. Hardness and luster
b. Color and cleavage
c. Cleavage and hardness
d. Luster and streak

14. Which of the following situations would produce the greatest change in motion?

a. The quarterback threw the regulation football using 50 Newtons of force.
b. The field goal kicker kicked the regulation football using 62 Newtons of force.
c. The coach tossed the regulation football using 21 Newtons of force.
d. The punter kicked the regulation football using 66 Newtons of force.

15. Students were given a science experiment to complete at home for homework over the weekend. The instructions they were given are shown below.

Evaporation Experiment
Please begin on Friday after school.
Question: Which evaporates faster, water or soda?
Procedure:

1. Pour ½ cup of soda in a 16 oz. clear jar.
2. Pour ½ cup of water in a 16 oz. clear jar.
3. Place both jars in a sunny location.
4. Mark the liquid level on the jar.
5. On Monday morning, mark the liquid level on the jar again.
6. Measure the distance between the two marks on each jar and record that data.

When students returned to class on Monday, most of the students determined that water evaporates faster. However, one student had the opposite results. Which statement below best explains why this might have happened?

a. The student worked with a partner from another class on the experiment.
b. The student used different measuring cups when measuring the ½ cup of liquid.
c. The student did not follow the procedures correctly.
d. The student placed the jars in a location that was too sunny.

16. Students were asked to create a closed circuit that would cause the bulb to light. One student created the circuits shown below.

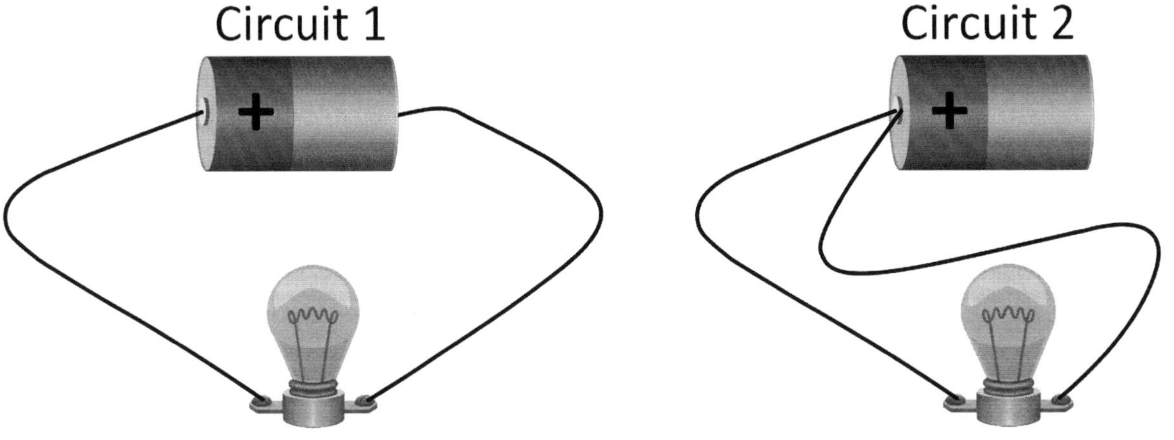

Which statement correctly describes both circuits made by the student?

a. Circuit 1 and circuit 2 both represent closed circuits because there are no gaps in the conducting wires. The light bulbs will light up on both circuits.
b. Circuit 1 represents a closed circuit, and the bulb will light. Circuit 2 does not represent a closed circuit and the bulb will not light because the conducting wires come from the same side of the power source.
c. Circuit 1 and circuit 2 both represent closed circuits, but neither will cause the bulb to light, since a switch is not present in either circuit.
d. Circuit 1 represents an open circuit since the conducting wires touch both sides of the power source. This will not cause the bulb to light. Circuit 2 represents a closed circuit and will cause the bulb to light.

17. Four windows are washed with different cleaners. The same paper towel is used on each. The squares below show each window before being cleaned. What is the independent variable in the experiment?

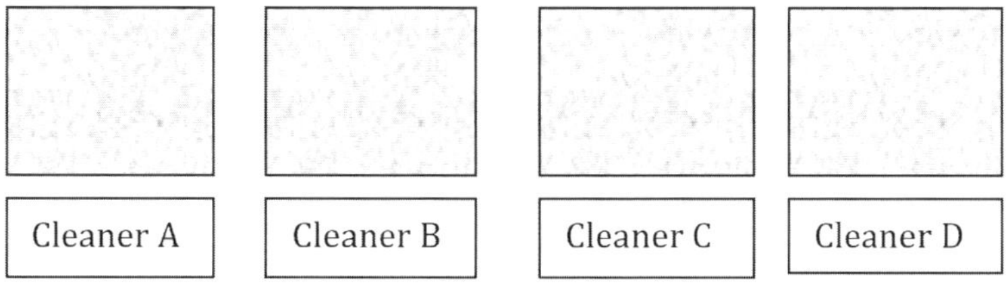

a. The amount of sunlight coming through the windows.
b. The type of window cleaner used.
c. The amount of dirt on each window.
d. The type of paper towel used.

18. The image below shows a popular Atlantic coast plant, sea oats.

Sea oats have tall stems and grow near sand dunes on the beaches of Florida. The sea oats in Florida have adapted to have a large root system that travels deep into the sand. How is the deep and complex root system an adaptation that helps the plant survive on the beaches in Florida?

a. The root system provides stability for the plant in windy conditions and loose sandy soil.
b. The deep root system helps the sea oats receive more freshwater than they would receive with shallow roots.
c. The complex root system helps the sea oats reproduce quickly and increase the population at a rapid rate.
d. The root system keeps humans from easily pulling up or interfering with the growth of the sea oats.

19. Students were asked to write a statement about both weathering and erosion. Which student best completed the assignment?

Student 1	The wind high up on a mountain slowly caused pieces of the mountain to break off.
Student 2	The tree roots pushed under the nearby sidewalk causing cracks.
Student 3	The river ran swiftly down the side of the mountain breaking off and carrying down bits of the mountain.
Student 4	The stream ran over the large boulders causing them to become smoother and smoother over time.

a. Student 1
b. Student 2
c. Student 3
d. Student 4

20. The science teacher asked the students to use the map below to write a comparison statement about the expected temperatures of two of the numbered areas below.

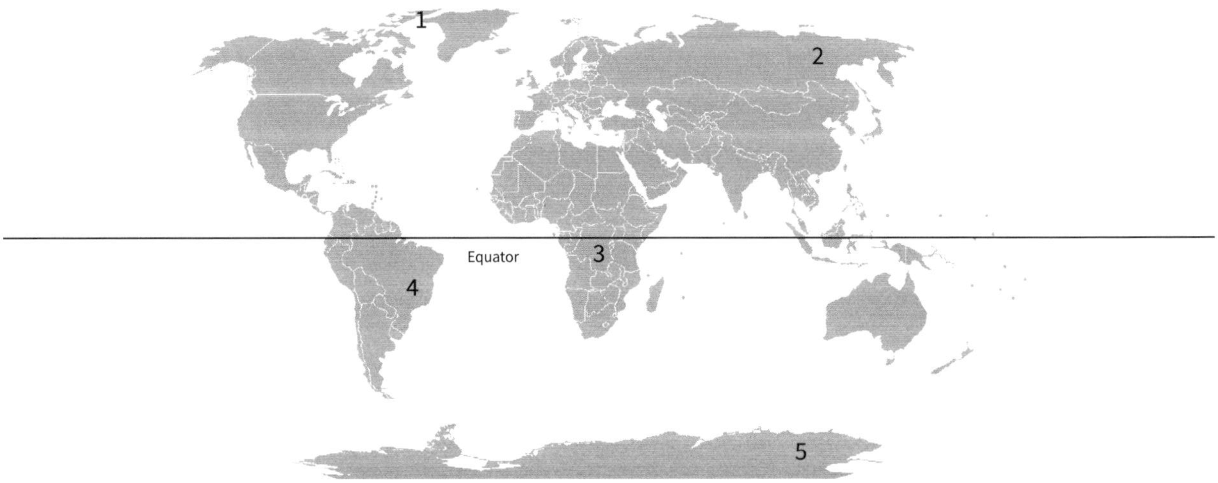

Which student wrote a statement that correctly compared the temperatures of two of the numbered areas on the map?

a. Student 1: Areas 2 and 5 would most likely have very similar temperatures throughout the year since they are both located in the eastern hemisphere of the world.
b. Student 2: Areas 3 and 4 would most likely have very different temperatures throughout the year since they are on different continents.
c. Student 3: Areas 1 and 4 would most likely have very similar temperatures throughout the year because they are both located near large bodies of water.
d. Student 4: Areas 1 and 3 would most likely have very different temperatures throughout the year because area 3 is right at the equator and area 1 is very far from the equator.

21. Ada conducts an experiment in which she tests how friction affects the movement of toy cars down an inclined plane.

Surface 1:

- Cover the incline plane with felt.
- Time the car as it goes down the incline plane.
- Repeat these two steps two more times.

Surface 2:

- Cover the incline plane with cotton.
- Time the car as it goes down the incline plane.
- Repeat these two steps two more times.

Surface 3:

- Cover the incline plane with silk.
- Time the car as it goes down the incline plane.
- Repeat these two steps two more times.

Why does Ada choose to send the car down the incline plane three different times for each of the fabric used?

a. Since there are three different types of fabric being tested, the experiment must be repeated three times.
b. Repeating an experiment produces information that is more valid and reliable.
c. If the experiment was not repeated, it would be impossible to be replicated by someone else.
d. It would be impossible to confirm the hypothesis without repeating the experiment.

22. What mistake was made in this chart that sorts conductors and insulators?

Conductors	Insulators
Copper	Glass
Iron	Rubber
Plastic	Wood
Steel	Cardboard

a. Wood is a conductor of electricity.
b. Steel and iron are insulators of electricity.
c. Plastic is an insulator of electricity.
d. Glass and rubber are conductors of electricity.

23. Two children are fighting over a teddy bear and are pulling on the bear in the direction of the arrows. The force child 1 uses to pull the bear is shown below.

Based on the picture above, which statement about the force and motion of the bear is true?

a. The bear will move in the direction of child 1 if child 2 pulls at a force greater than 20 newtons.
b. The bear will move in the direction of child 1 if the force child 2 uses is equal to the force used by child 1.
c. The bear will not move if child 2 uses a force of exactly 20 newtons when pulling the bear.
d. The bear will move in the direction of child 2 if the force child 2 uses is less than 20 newtons.

24. Which statement correctly completes the chart shown below?

Solar System Object	Fact
Sun	A star that is orbited by the Earth
Moons	________________
Asteroids	Rocky objects smaller than planets that orbit the Sun
Planets	Spherical in shape and orbit the Sun

a. A frozen ball of gas and rock that revolves around the Sun
b. A round object that revolves around the planet it belongs to
c. Celestial objects that revolve around the sun every month
d. The largest objects in the Milky Way galaxy

25. Lions live in savannah and grassland regions where there are tall dry grasses. Lions must sneak up and stalk their prey. What is the most likely reason for a lion's sand colored coat?

a. It allows lions to hide within the grass.
b. The light color of their coat reflects heat from the Sun.
c. A lion's coloring helps it attract mates.
d. It allows them to run faster than their prey.

Answer Key and Explanations for Test #3

1. B: SC.5.L.14.2

The exoskeleton of an apple snail protects the snail's inner organs like the bark protects the inner parts of the live oak tree. The gills of the sailfish help the fish to breathe in water, the feathers help the blue heron fly, and the claws of the Florida black bear assist in killing prey.

2. B: SC.4.P.12.1

An object like a baseball is in motion when there is a change in the object's position. A mass change would not indicate that an object moved. A frictional change or a gravitational change would affect the motion of an object, but neither is required for an object to be considered in motion.

3. D: SC.5.P.9.1

Student 4 is correct because a chemical reaction occurred when the log turned to ash. This chemical change occurred when heat from the fire was added to the log. Student 1 is incorrect because morning dew is an example of a physical change and occurs when water vapor in the air is cooled. Student 2 is incorrect because hammering a bowl with a heated mallet is an example of a physical change. Student 3 is incorrect because water from the snow caused the chemical change that formed the rust, not the cold temperature of the snow.

4. C: SC.5.E.5.1

It is not true that planets are not a part of galaxies. Planets like Earth are a part of the Milky Way galaxy. Galaxies are made up of many stars, gases, dust, and other objects, like planets, that orbit stars.

5. B: SC.3.L.15.1

Lobsters are invertebrates like crabs and shrimp, meaning they don't have a backbone. Sea otters, whales, and seals are vertebrates, meaning they do have a backbone.

6. B: SC.5.E.7.1

Water droplets forming on the side of an icy cup perfectly illustrate the process of condensation as the icy cup cools the water vapor in the air and turns that water vapor back into small drops of liquid water. Heating a pot of water with a hot pot or heating a tank of water with a heat lamp would model the process of evaporation. Dropping small drops of water into a tray would model precipitation and collection.

7. B: SC.4.P.10.3

A higher pitch on a guitar can be produced by tightening the strings so that the vibrations of the strings move faster. The faster the strings vibrate the higher the pitch becomes. Slowing down the vibrations will decrease the pitch. Longer strings would slow the vibration and lower the pitch.

8. A: SC.5.N.2.1

Consistent measuring devices must be used when recording the data in the experiment for it to be considered valid. Basic observations or the use of nonstandard measuring tools will not result in reliable evidence that can be tested again. It is not necessary to start a science experiment with a question or hypothesis. Completing the experiment more than once would make the experiment more valid.

9. B: SC.3.L.14.1

The function of flowers is to produce pollen and attract pollinators that will help the plant reproduce and create more plants just like it. The leaves on a plant use nutrients and sunlight to make food for the plant through the process of photosynthesis. The stem of the plant moves nutrients and provides stability. The roots of the plant absorb water and other nutrients from the ground.

10. A: SC.5.L.14.1

The spinal cord is the pathway where messages are sent to and from the brain in the human body. These organs work together to send and receive signals to and from various parts of the body. One would not work without the other. The lungs are responsible for breathing, and the stomach is apart of digestion. The heart pumps blood while the bladder holds urine. The eyes aid in sight, and the pancreas makes digestive fluids.

11. C: SC.5.N.1.6

Noting the mixture foaming and rising in the container is the observation because it is a fact regarding something that happened during the experiment. It is not an opinion or belief but can be verified by anyone who also completes the experiment. The excitement or difficulty level of the experiment relates to someone's opinion and is not true for everyone who completes the experiment. Someone's expectations for how quickly something occurred is how they interpret the experiment, but this is not true for everyone completing the experiment.

12. C: SC.5.E.7.3

The lowest humidity for the coastal area did occur on Monday, but the lowest humidity for the inland area occurred on Wednesday. This is the statement that is not true. The highest humidity for both areas did occur on Tuesday. The humidity in the coastal area was always greater than the humidity in the inland area and therefore, the humidity in the inland area was always the lowest during the three days.

13. D: SC.4.E.6.2

The students are exploring the luster of the minerals when they observe the shiny or dull nature of the mineral. The students are exploring streak when they rub the mineral on a white piece of cardboard and notice the color left behind. Hardness would be observed by attempting to scratch the mineral. Color is observed by viewing the color of the mineral. Cleavage is observed by noticing how the mineral breaks.

14. D: SC.5.P.13.2

The greatest change in motion of the football would occur when the most force is applied to the regulation football, which in this example was 66 Newtons of force. Less force is applied to the football in all of the other options and would result in a smaller change in motion.

15. C: SC.5.N.2.2

When the procedures to an experiment are not followed correctly, inaccurate and unreliable results can occur. The other students were able to replicate this experiment correctly because they followed the procedures correctly. Working with a partner, measuring ½ using different measuring cups, and placing the jars in an extra sunny location do not change the procedures of the experiment and would not affect the results.

16. B: SC.5.P.11.1

Circuit 1 represents a closed circuit since the conducting wires come from the positive side of the power source, move through both sides of the light bulb and to the negative side of the power source. This closed circuit will cause the bulb to light. Circuit 2 does not represent a closed circuit because although there are no breaks in the conducting wires, the wires never complete the circuit by attaching to the negative end of the power source. Circuit 2 will not cause the bulb to light. Switches are sometimes part of circuits, but they are not needed for the circuit to work correctly.

17. B: SC.5.N.1.1

An independent variable is something that is changed in the experiment. It is being tested against other similar things. In this experiment, the independent variable is the type of window cleaner.

18. A: SC.4.L.16.2

The windy conditions and loose sandy soil at the beach create an environment where the sea oats could be uprooted easily. The plant has adapted to grow a deep and complex root system to provide stability and keep the plant in the ground. The roots do not provide freshwater for the sea oats since it is near the ocean. The roots are not responsible for reproduction and do not prevent human interference.

19. C: SC.4.E.6.4

Student 3 is the only student who explains both weathering and erosion. Weathering refers to the rock breaking down and erosion refers to the rocks carried down the mountain. The other students only gave an example of weathering but not erosion, because they did not discuss the weathered pieces being moved somewhere else.

20. D: SC.5.E.7.6

Areas located close to the equator have much warmer temperatures than areas that are far away from the equator. Area 3 is located along the equator so temperatures in that location are very warm. Area 1 is located far north of the equator and would therefore have cold temperatures. Being in the same hemisphere does not mean that areas will have similar temperatures. Areas on different continents can have similar temperatures if the areas are both located relatively the same distance from the equator. Being close to large bodies of water does not mean the areas would have similar temperatures.

21. B: SC.5.N.1.3

Repeating the timing of the car three times for each type of fabric creates more valid results and eliminates user errors that might affect the data gathered. The number of variables, such as the number of different fabrics being used, does not determine how many times an experiment should be repeated. Experiments do not have to be repeated to be replicated. They just have to be recorded and explained clearly. Although repetition leads to a more reliable answer to a hypothesis, a hypothesis could be formed without repetition.

22. C: SC.5.P.11.2

Copper, iron, and steel are all good conductors of electricity, but plastic does not conduct electricity and should be in the insulator column. Glass, rubber, wood, and cardboard are all insulators and don't allow electricity to travel through them easily.

23. C: SC.5.P.13.4

Since child 1 is using a force of 20 newtons to pull on the bear, if child 2 uses exactly 20 newtons to pull the other direction on the bear, there will be a balanced force and the bear will not move. If child 2 pulls with a greater force than the 20 newtons child one is using, the bear would move in the direction of child 2. If child 2 pulls with a force less than 20 newtons, the bear would move in the direction of child 1.

24. B: SC.5.E.5.3

Moons are round objects, and moons always revolve around the planets they belong to. Option A is describing the definition of a comet. Moons do not revolve around the sun every month, and they are not the largest objects in our galaxy.

25. A: SC.5.L.17.1

Lions live in a wide open area where there are few large objects to hide behind. In order to get close enough to their prey to chase and attack it, they must be able to sneak up on it. Their coloration is similar to the color of the tall grasses where they live. This allows the lions to blend into their surroundings and get close to their prey.

Practice Test #4

1. Students are asked to write a report about a small object that revolves around a larger planet. What topic are the students writing about?

a. Stars
b. Comets
c. Asteroids
d. Moons

2. A student is working on creating a model of the water cycle to present to her science class. The student pours water into half of a five-gallon clear bucket and then places a clear lid on top of the bucket like the picture below.

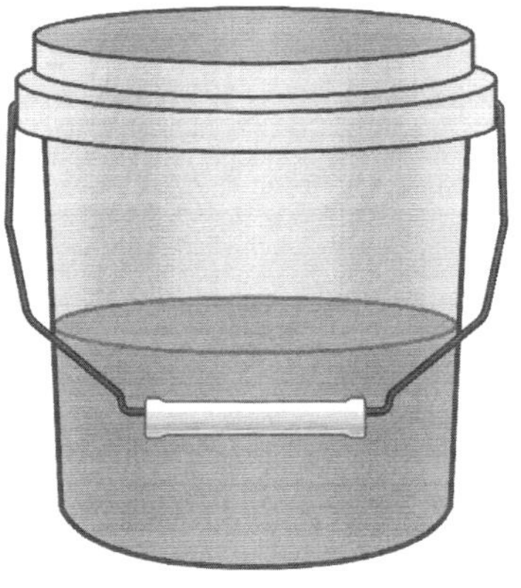

What could be added to the model to allow evaporation to occur?

a. A bag of ice
b. A container of water
c. A heat lamp
d. A small fan

3. The Florida leafwing has beautiful orange coloring on the inside of its wings that can be seen during flight. However, when the leafwing lands and closes its wings, they are a gray color that resembles the branches in a tree. How does this coloring benefit the Florida leafwing?

a. The orange coloring allows the leafwing to blend in with the flowers in the area.
b. The gray coloring provides camouflage to protect the leafwing from predators when it lands.
c. The coloring changes allow the leafwing to confuse its predator into thinking it is two different creatures.
d. The coloring allows other leafwings to find each other more easily.

4. Wetlands, like those found in the Everglades in Florida, are warm areas with access to plenty of water which create very humid conditions. Which area would have a climate most unlike the wetlands?

a. Tundra
b. Rainforests
c. Coastal regions
d. Tropical areas

5. Students are conducting an experiment outside on the playground using a baseball, basketball, playground ball, and a tennis ball. The teacher climbs up a ladder and is given a certain type of ball by a student. The teacher then drops the ball from the top of the ladder as students count the number of times the ball touches the ground and moves back up into the air before coming to a complete stop. The students record the data on their observation charts. Which of the following questions might the students be trying to answer?

a. Which type of ball reaches the ground the fastest?
b. Which type of ball bounces the highest?
c. Which type of ball is the bounciest?
d. Which type of ball creates the least amount of friction?

6. Slash pine trees and peach trees both grow in various places in Florida.

Which part of the lifecycle of the slash pine tree is most like the fruit in the lifecycle of the peach tree?

a. The pine needles
b. The seedling
c. The cone
d. The flowers

7. Students are working to identify three unknown substances. Their observations are shown below.

Observable Property	Substance 1	Substance 2	Substance 3
Has fixed volume?	Yes	No	Yes
Color	Green	Yellow	Red
Takes shape of container?	No	Yes	No
Mass	300 grams	287 grams	129 grams

Based on the students' observations, which substance(s) are most likely solid(s)?

a. Substance 1 only
b. Substances 1 and 2
c. Substances 1, 2, and 3
d. Substances 1 and 3

8. Students were asked to write a paragraph about a time they saw energy creating a change during a sporting event. The students submitted the following topics to the teacher. Which topic does NOT illustrate energy creating a change?

Topic 1: The baseball soared into right field after the batter hit it with the bat.
Topic 2: The player threw the basketball up to the hoop, but it rolled off the rim.
Topic 3: The soccer ball sat in the middle of the field before the game started.
Topic 4: The football flew straight threw the middle of the goal post after the player kicked it.

a. Topic 1
b. Topic 2
c. Topic 3
d. Topic 4

9. The science teacher asked the students in her class to write one fact about scientific investigations. The student responses are shown below.

Student 1: An authentic scientific investigation does not have to follow all steps in the scientific method, but it does have to start with a hypothesis.
Student 2: To be an authentic scientific investigation all steps of the scientific process must be followed but can be followed in any order.
Student 3: The steps of the scientific method do not have to be followed for an authentic scientific investigation to happen.

Which student(s) wrote a fact about scientific investigations that is completely correct?

a. Student 1 only
b. Student 1 and 2
c. Student 2 only
d. Student 3 only

10. Mrs. Smith asked the students to write four facts describing the relationship of the Sun, Moon, Earth, and stars. Andrea wrote the statements below.

1. The Sun moves across the Earth sky each day as it passes over different parts of the Earth.
2. The Earth rotates on its axis causing the Sun to look like it is moving across the sky even though it doesn't move.
3. The moon rotates around the Sun causing the Sun to look like it moves across the sky during the day.
4. Since the Earth rotates on its axis we see the same stars every single night.

Which statement is the only one that is completely correct?

a. Statement 1
b. Statement 2
c. Statement 3
d. Statement 4

11. Dedra is a picky eater. She separated her trail mix at lunch because she wanted to eat each item separately. She used her hands to sort the pretzels, marshmallows, and cereal. What other mixture could be sorted in the same way?

a. Sugar and salt
b. Iron filling and sand
c. Nails and screws
d. Garlic salt and pepper

12. Students were asked to write one fact about the food chain shown below.

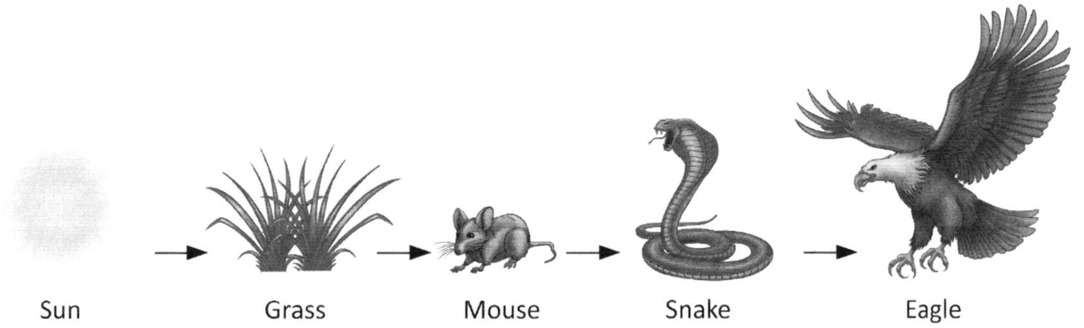

Which statement about the food chain is NOT correct?

a. Energy is transferred from the snake to the eagle.
b. The sun's energy is transferred to the grass.
c. The grass is a consumer.
d. The mouse provides energy for the snake.

13. Blood is moved throughout the body in arteries and veins. What human organ pumps blood so that it can be moved by arteries and veins?

a. Lungs
b. Liver
c. Pancreas
d. Heart

14. Alex and Robert's science fair project investigates the effect of different liquids on surfaces like teeth. The boys use seashells instead of teeth in the experiment since they are made of very similar substances. Part of their science fair board is shown below.

The Effect of Different Drinks on Teeth

Question: How do different drinks affect teeth?
(Seashells will be used to represent teeth in this experiment.)

Procedure: Put a seashell in a container of water, a container of coke, and a container of sports drink. Observe the shell in each container twice a week for one month.

Explanation: The soda had the greatest impact on the shell.

What major component of science is missing from their board?

a. More than three different variables should have been tested to make the explanation more reliable.
b. There must be a description of the observations and evidence to back up the explanation.
c. The students must include a hypothesis for it to represent true science.
d. It must be shown that the experiment was completed at least three times to make the explanation valid.

15. Miguel is cooking pasta on the stove. He pours two cups of water in the pot, adds the pasta, places the pot on the stove, and turns it on. After ten minutes, Miguel notices steam rising from the pot. Why is this happening?

a. The pasta at the bottom of the pot was burning, causing smoke to rise from the pot.
b. The water in the pot was heated and is evaporating, causing water vapor to rise from the pot.
c. The heat under the pot is too hot, creating steam.
d. The steam forms as the water cools after the pasta is finished cooking.

16. Students were asked to complete the chart below.

Energy Transfer	Example
Electrical to sound	Television
Electrical to heat	Toaster
Electrical to light	________________

Which example belongs in the blank?

a. Hair dryer
b. Lamp
c. Solar panel
d. Speaker

17. The students had to classify different plants into those that make seeds and those that make spores. The teacher gave the example below of an orange tree producing seeds and moss producing spores.

Seeds

Spores

Which other plant would belong in the spore category?

a. Fern

b. Apple tree

c. Hibiscus

d. Dogwood

18. The baseball player hit the baseball causing it to fly into center field and then fall to the ground. Which correctly describes the force that caused the ball to fall to the ground?

a. The push off the bat
b. The pull of gravity
c. The push of the air
d. The pull of friction

19. Which of the following statements about the Milky Way galaxy is correct?

a. The Milky Way galaxy contains the inner planet Mercury, but not the outer planet Jupiter.
b. The Milky Way galaxy contains the Earth, Sun, and other planets in our solar system.
c. The Milky Way galaxy is too dangerous to be explored by astronauts.
d. The Milky Way galaxy is too far away to even be seen with a telescope.

20. When Andrew was getting ready for bed, he set his digital alarm clock to wake him up at 6:00 the next morning. What are the two types of energy that the alarm clock uses?

a. Electrical and sound
b. Thermal and chemical
c. Chemical and electrical
d. Mechanical and thermal

21. Apple trees grow well in the moist environment of northern Florida.

The bark on the apple tree has a similar function to what human organ?

a. Lungs
b. Skin
c. Brain
d. Large intestine

22. Students in Mrs. Peterson's class recorded different weather conditions in three different areas. Their data is displayed in the table below.

	Area 1	Area 2	Area 3
Temperature	85°F	82°F	90°F
Precipitation	5 cm	2 cm	4 cm
Humidity	85%	50%	60%
Wind	3 mph from the North	4 mph from the West	4 mph from the East

Which statement about the weather is true for all three areas?

a. There are dangerously high winds in all three areas.
b. It will be a snowy day for all three areas.
c. Citizens living in these areas should wear a large coat.
d. The precipitation expected in all three areas will be rain.

23. Florida has many renewable and nonrenewable resources that its citizens use every day. Which list below only contains nonrenewable resources?

a. Wind, sunlight, water, oxygen
b. Wind, limestone, coal, oxygen
c. Limestone, petroleum, coal, water
d. Limestone, aluminum, petroleum, coal

24. Florida is a peninsula in the Gulf of Mexico and Atlantic Ocean. Which statement is true about areas near large bodies of water?

a. Areas near large bodies of water have much colder temperatures than areas further away from water.
b. Areas near large bodies of water receive more rain than areas further away from water.
c. Areas near large bodies of water have warmer temperatures than areas further away from water.
d. Areas near large bodies of water are drier than areas further away from water.

25. Which of the following practices would be the least important to consider when designing and conducting an experiment that can be easily replicated by others?

a. Creating a clear hypothesis.
b. Writing detailed instructions about the exact type and brand of materials used.
c. Using a measuring device when adding materials to the experiment.
d. Record all the steps to the experiment clearly.

Answer Key and Explanations for Test #4

1. D: SC.5.E.5.3

Moons are small space objects that revolve around a larger planet. Stars are huge balls of burning gases and do not revolve around planets. Asteroids and comets revolve around the Sun, which is a star.

2. C: SC.5.E.7.1

Adding a heat lamp will warm the water and cause evaporation to occur. Adding a bag of ice to the top of the bucket would cool the water vapor in the air, which would create condensation on the lid of the bucket. A container of water would not cause evaporation to occur. A small fan might aid in evaporation in exposed water, but not water in a bucket with a lid.

3. B: SC.5.L.17.1

The gray coloring on the outside of the leafwing's wings allows it to camouflage itself when landing on tree branches which protects it from predators. The orange is on the inside of the wings so if it lands on a flower, the orange will not be visible. The coloring differences would not confuse a predator nor allow the leafwings to be detected by each other more easily.

4. A: SC.5.E.7.5

A tundra are very cold areas on the top of mountains where it is windy and dry with little humidity. Rainforests are dark, humid, and full of moisture because of the different levels in a rainforest. Coastal regions are near water which, when evaporated, adds lots of moisture and humidity to the air. Tropical regions tend to be near the equator and are therefore warmer causing more evaporation and more humidity in the air.

5. C: SC.5.N.1.1

The students are counting the number of bounces for each ball the teacher drops since they are counting the number of times the ball touches the ground and then moves back up into the air before stopping. They are trying to answer the question, "Which type of ball is the bounciest?" They are not trying to determine which ball reaches the ground the fastest since they are not timing the drops. They are also not measuring the height of the bounce or measuring friction.

6. C: SC.4.L.16.4

The peach on the peach tree produces the seed that is required to restart the lifecycle of the peach tree, and the cone on the slash pine produces the seed that is required to grow a new slash pine. The seedling is what grows from the seeds. The pine needles are most like the leaves on the peach tree. The slash pine produces cones, not flowers.

7. D: SC.5.P.8.1

Substances 1 and 3 both have a fixed volume and do not take the shape of their containers, which are factors consistent with solid materials. The mass and color columns do not help to differentiate between solids and liquids. Substance 2 cannot be a solid because it does not have a fixed volume, and it takes the shape of its container.

8. C: SC.5.P.10.2

The soccer ball never changed or moved so it does not illustrate energy creating a change. The baseball bat hit the baseball, the basketball player threw the basketball, and the football player kicked the football which all illustrate energy creating a change in the position of the ball.

9. D: SC.5.N.1.5

An authentic scientific investigation does not have to follow the steps of the scientific method because simple observations can be considered a scientific investigation. Student 1 is incorrect because scientific investigations do not have to start with a hypothesis, and Student 2 is incorrect because the steps of the scientific method do not have to be followed.

10. B: SC.4.E.5.4

Statement 2 is the only statement that is correct because the Sun looks like it moves across the sky due to the Earth rotating on its axis. The Sun does not actually move, it is stationary. The moon revolves around the Earth, but it does not rotate around the Sun. Since the Earth rotates on its axis, we see different stars during different times of the year.

11. C: SC.5.P.8.3

Dedra used her hands to separate the trail mix, and the nail and screw mixture is the only other mixture listed that can be separated in this way. The other mixtures contain ingredients that are too small to be separated by hand.

12. C: SC.4.L.17.3

The grass is a producer because it makes its own food using energy from the sun. It is not a consumer because it does not consume an organism to gain energy. The snake provides energy to the eagle when the eagle consumes the snake. The sun is what gives the grass energy to make its own food. The mouse provides energy for the snake when it is consumed by the snake.

13. D: SC.5.L.14.1

The heart is the organ that pumps blood through the arteries and veins in the human body. The lungs are used for breathing and the liver and pancreas are organs that help humans digest food.

14. B: SC.5.N.2.1

True, reliable science is always backed up by evidence based on observations. The explanation cannot be made without evidence to prove why the explanation is true. A true scientific investigation does not have to have a certain number of variables. A hypothesis is not always required in scientific experiments and explanations. Although repetition does create more reliable results, it is not required.

15. B: SC.5.P.9.1

When the water in the pot was heated, it began to evaporate and can be seen as steam. The steam would not be caused by burnt pasta or overheating. Steam does not form as water cools, but instead as water is heated.

16. B: SC.5.P.10.4

When a lamp is plugged into an electrical socket, it transfers electrical energy to light energy. A hair dryer transfers electrical energy to heat energy. A speaker transfers electrical energy to sound energy. Solar panels transfer energy from light into electrical energy, not electrical energy into light energy.

17. A: SC.3.L.15.2

As you can see from the picture, the fern produces spores similar to that of the moss. The apple tree, hibiscus, and dogwood all produce flowers that make seeds, which is similar to the orange tree in the example picture.

18. B: SC.5.P.13.1

Gravity is the force that pulled the baseball to the ground. The push of the bat is what sent the baseball flying through the air. The push of the air may cause the ball to go further. There may have been some friction at play, but this would not cause the ball to fall to the ground.

19. B: SC.5.E.5.1

The Milky Way galaxy is the name of our galaxy and contains the Earth, the Sun, and the other planets that orbit the Sun. The Milky Way galaxy contains all the other celestial objects in our solar system as well. The Milky Way galaxy has been explored by astronauts and can be observed with a telescope.

20. A: SC.5.P.10.1

The digital alarm clock uses electrical energy because it must be plugged into an electrical source to work. Sound energy is produced when the alarm sounds to alert the sleeping person. Thermal and mechanical energy is not used or produced by the alarm clock. Chemical energy is not used because the alarm clock runs off electricity.

21. B: SC.5.L.14.2

The bark on an apple tree provides protection to the tree like the way the skin provides protection to the human body. The lungs are responsible for respiration, the brain sends signals throughout the body, and the large intestine aids digestion.

22. D: SC.5.E.7.3

Rain would be the expected precipitation since the temperatures in all three areas are very warm. The wind speed for all the areas is very low, so the winds would not be dangerous. The temperatures are all very warm, so citizens would not need to wear coats and snow would not be possible with the temperatures well above freezing.

23. D: SC.4.E.6.3

Limestone, aluminum, petroleum, and coal are all substances that are natural to the Earth but will eventually run out and cannot be replaced while we are alive. Wind, sunlight, water, and oxygen can be renewed and will never run out during our lifetime.

24. B: SC.5.E.7.6

Areas near large bodies of water receive more rainfall than areas further away from water. The large bodies of water add a lot of moisture to the air which results in more rainfall. Areas near water can have warmer or colder climates depending on their distance from the equator. Areas near water are wetter, not drier, than other areas.

25. A: SC.5.N.2.2

Creating a clear hypothesis would be the least important in designing an experiment that can be easily replicated because the hypothesis does not affect the experiment in any way. It is simply the scientist's prediction of the results of the experiment. Communicating the exact type and brand of the materials in the experiment will help it to be replicated more accurately. Using a measuring device when adding materials to the experiment will help it be more easily replicated because the same amounts can be used each time. For an experiment to be replicated successfully, it is very important that all the steps are recorded clearly.

How to Overcome Test Anxiety

Just the thought of taking a test is enough to make most people a little nervous. A test is an important event that can have a long-term impact on your future, so it's important to take it seriously and it's natural to feel anxious about performing well. But just because anxiety is normal, that doesn't mean that it's helpful in test taking, or that you should simply accept it as part of your life. Anxiety can have a variety of effects. These effects can be mild, like making you feel slightly nervous, or severe, like blocking your ability to focus or remember even a simple detail.

If you experience test anxiety—whether severe or mild—it's important to know how to beat it. To discover this, first you need to understand what causes test anxiety.

Causes of Test Anxiety

While we often think of anxiety as an uncontrollable emotional state, it can actually be caused by simple, practical things. One of the most common causes of test anxiety is that a person does not feel adequately prepared for their test. This feeling can be the result of many different issues such as poor study habits or lack of organization, but the most common culprit is time management. Starting to study too late, failing to organize your study time to cover all of the material, or being distracted while you study will mean that you're not well prepared for the test. This may lead to cramming the night before, which will cause you to be physically and mentally exhausted for the test. Poor time management also contributes to feelings of stress, fear, and hopelessness as you realize you are not well prepared but don't know what to do about it.

Other times, test anxiety is not related to your preparation for the test but comes from unresolved fear. This may be a past failure on a test, or poor performance on tests in general. It may come from comparing yourself to others who seem to be performing better or from the stress of living up to expectations. Anxiety may be driven by fears of the future—how failure on this test would affect your educational and career goals. These fears are often completely irrational, but they can still negatively impact your test performance.

Elements of Test Anxiety

As mentioned earlier, test anxiety is considered to be an emotional state, but it has physical and mental components as well. Sometimes you may not even realize that you are suffering from test anxiety until you notice the physical symptoms. These can include trembling hands, rapid heartbeat, sweating, nausea, and tense muscles. Extreme anxiety may lead to fainting or vomiting. Obviously, any of these symptoms can have a negative impact on testing. It is important to recognize them as soon as they begin to occur so that you can address the problem before it damages your performance.

The mental components of test anxiety include trouble focusing and inability to remember learned information. During a test, your mind is on high alert, which can help you recall information and stay focused for an extended period of time. However, anxiety interferes with your mind's natural processes, causing you to blank out, even on the questions you know well. The strain of testing during anxiety makes it difficult to stay focused, especially on a test that may take several hours. Extreme anxiety can take a huge mental toll, making it difficult not only to recall test information but even to understand the test questions or pull your thoughts together.

Effects of Test Anxiety

Test anxiety is like a disease—if left untreated, it will get progressively worse. Anxiety leads to poor performance, and this reinforces the feelings of fear and failure, which in turn lead to poor performances on subsequent tests. It can grow from a mild nervousness to a crippling condition. If allowed to progress, test anxiety can have a big impact on your schooling, and consequently on your future.

Test anxiety can spread to other parts of your life. Anxiety on tests can become anxiety in any stressful situation, and blanking on a test can turn into panicking in a job situation. But fortunately, you don't have to let anxiety rule your testing and determine your grades. There are a number of relatively simple steps you can take to move past anxiety and function normally on a test and in the rest of life.

Physical Steps for Beating Test Anxiety

While test anxiety is a serious problem, the good news is that it can be overcome. It doesn't have to control your ability to think and remember information. While it may take time, you can begin taking steps today to beat anxiety.

Just as your first hint that you may be struggling with anxiety comes from the physical symptoms, the first step to treating it is also physical. Rest is crucial for having a clear, strong mind. If you are tired, it is much easier to give in to anxiety. But if you establish good sleep habits, your body and mind will be ready to perform optimally, without the strain of exhaustion. Additionally, sleeping well helps you to retain information better, so you're more likely to recall the answers when you see the test questions.

Getting good sleep means more than going to bed on time. It's important to allow your brain time to relax. Take study breaks from time to time so it doesn't get overworked, and don't study right before bed. Take time to rest your mind before trying to rest your body, or you may find it difficult to fall asleep.

Along with sleep, other aspects of physical health are important in preparing for a test. Good nutrition is vital for good brain function. Sugary foods and drinks may give a burst of energy but this burst is followed by a crash, both physically and emotionally. Instead, fuel your body with protein and vitamin-rich foods.

Also, drink plenty of water. Dehydration can lead to headaches and exhaustion, especially if your brain is already under stress from the rigors of the test. Particularly if your test is a long one, drink water during the breaks. And if possible, take an energy-boosting snack to eat between sections.

Along with sleep and diet, a third important part of physical health is exercise. Maintaining a steady workout schedule is helpful, but even taking 5-minute study breaks to walk can help get your blood pumping faster and clear your head. Exercise also releases endorphins, which contribute to a positive feeling and can help combat test anxiety.

When you nurture your physical health, you are also contributing to your mental health. If your body is healthy, your mind is much more likely to be healthy as well. So take time to rest, nourish your body with healthy food and water, and get moving as much as possible. Taking these physical steps will make you stronger and more able to take the mental steps necessary to overcome test anxiety.

Mental Steps for Beating Test Anxiety

Working on the mental side of test anxiety can be more challenging, but as with the physical side, there are clear steps you can take to overcome it. As mentioned earlier, test anxiety often stems from lack of preparation, so the obvious solution is to prepare for the test. Effective studying may be the most important weapon you have for beating test anxiety, but you can and should employ several other mental tools to combat fear.

First, boost your confidence by reminding yourself of past success—tests or projects that you aced. If you're putting as much effort into preparing for this test as you did for those, there's no reason you should expect to fail here. Work hard to prepare; then trust your preparation.

Second, surround yourself with encouraging people. It can be helpful to find a study group, but be sure that the people you're around will encourage a positive attitude. If you spend time with others who are anxious or cynical, this will only contribute to your own anxiety. Look for others who are motivated to study hard from a desire to succeed, not from a fear of failure.

Third, reward yourself. A test is physically and mentally tiring, even without anxiety, and it can be helpful to have something to look forward to. Plan an activity following the test, regardless of the outcome, such as going to a movie or getting ice cream.

When you are taking the test, if you find yourself beginning to feel anxious, remind yourself that you know the material. Visualize successfully completing the test. Then take a few deep, relaxing breaths and return to it. Work through the questions carefully but with confidence, knowing that you are capable of succeeding.

Developing a healthy mental approach to test taking will also aid in other areas of life. Test anxiety affects more than just the actual test—it can be damaging to your mental health and even contribute to depression. It's important to beat test anxiety before it becomes a problem for more than testing.

Study Strategy

Being prepared for the test is necessary to combat anxiety, but what does being prepared look like? You may study for hours on end and still not feel prepared. What you need is a strategy for test prep. The next few pages outline our recommended steps to help you plan out and conquer the challenge of preparation.

Step 1: Scope Out the Test

Learn everything you can about the format (multiple choice, essay, etc.) and what will be on the test. Gather any study materials, course outlines, or sample exams that may be available. Not only will this help you to prepare, but knowing what to expect can help to alleviate test anxiety.

Step 2: Map Out the Material

Look through the textbook or study guide and make note of how many chapters or sections it has. Then divide these over the time you have. For example, if a book has 15 chapters and you have five days to study, you need to cover three chapters each day. Even better, if you have the time, leave an extra day at the end for overall review after you have gone through the material in depth.

If time is limited, you may need to prioritize the material. Look through it and make note of which sections you think you already have a good grasp on, and which need review. While you are studying, skim quickly through the familiar sections and take more time on the challenging parts.

Write out your plan so you don't get lost as you go. Having a written plan also helps you feel more in control of the study, so anxiety is less likely to arise from feeling overwhelmed at the amount to cover.

Step 3: Gather Your Tools

Decide what study method works best for you. Do you prefer to highlight in the book as you study and then go back over the highlighted portions? Or do you type out notes of the important information? Or is it helpful to make flashcards that you can carry with you? Assemble the pens, index cards, highlighters, post-it notes, and any other materials you may need so you won't be distracted by getting up to find things while you study.

If you're having a hard time retaining the information or organizing your notes, experiment with different methods. For example, try color-coding by subject with colored pens, highlighters, or post-it notes. If you learn better by hearing, try recording yourself reading your notes so you can listen while in the car, working out, or simply sitting at your desk. Ask a friend to quiz you from your flashcards, or try teaching someone the material to solidify it in your mind.

Step 4: Create Your Environment

It's important to avoid distractions while you study. This includes both the obvious distractions like visitors and the subtle distractions like an uncomfortable chair (or a too-comfortable couch that makes you want to fall asleep). Set up the best study environment possible: good lighting and a comfortable work area. If background music helps you focus, you may want to turn it on, but otherwise keep the room quiet. If you are using a computer to take notes, be sure you don't have any other windows open, especially applications like social media, games, or anything else that could distract you. Silence your phone and turn off notifications. Be sure to keep water close by so you stay hydrated while you study (but avoid unhealthy drinks and snacks).

Also, take into account the best time of day to study. Are you freshest first thing in the morning? Try to set aside some time then to work through the material. Is your mind clearer in the afternoon or evening? Schedule your study session then. Another method is to study at the same time of day that you will take the test, so that your brain gets used to working on the material at that time and will be ready to focus at test time.

Step 5: Study!

Once you have done all the study preparation, it's time to settle into the actual studying. Sit down, take a few moments to settle your mind so you can focus, and begin to follow your study plan. Don't give in to distractions or let yourself procrastinate. This is your time to prepare so you'll be ready to fearlessly approach the test. Make the most of the time and stay focused.

Of course, you don't want to burn out. If you study too long you may find that you're not retaining the information very well. Take regular study breaks. For example, taking five minutes out of every hour to walk briskly, breathing deeply and swinging your arms, can help your mind stay fresh.

As you get to the end of each chapter or section, it's a good idea to do a quick review. Remind yourself of what you learned and work on any difficult parts. When you feel that you've mastered the material, move on to the next part. At the end of your study session, briefly skim through your notes again.

But while review is helpful, cramming last minute is NOT. If at all possible, work ahead so that you won't need to fit all your study into the last day. Cramming overloads your brain with more information than it can process and retain, and your tired mind may struggle to recall even previously learned information when it is overwhelmed with last-minute study. Also, the urgent nature of cramming and the stress placed on your brain contribute to anxiety. You'll be more likely to go to the test feeling unprepared and having trouble thinking clearly.

So don't cram, and don't stay up late before the test, even just to review your notes at a leisurely pace. Your brain needs rest more than it needs to go over the information again. In fact, plan to finish your studies by noon or early afternoon the day before the test. Give your brain the rest of the day to relax or focus on other things, and get a good night's sleep. Then you will be fresh for the test and better able to recall what you've studied.

Step 6: Take a Practice Test

Many courses offer sample tests, either online or in the study materials. This is an excellent resource to check whether you have mastered the material, as well as to prepare for the test format and environment.

Check the test format ahead of time: the number of questions, the type (multiple choice, free response, etc.), and the time limit. Then create a plan for working through them. For example, if you have 30 minutes to take a 60-question test, your limit is 30 seconds per question. Spend less time on the questions you know well so that you can take more time on the difficult ones.

If you have time to take several practice tests, take the first one open book, with no time limit. Work through the questions at your own pace and make sure you fully understand them. Gradually work up to taking a test under test conditions: sit at a desk with all study materials put away and set a timer. Pace yourself to make sure you finish the test with time to spare and go back to check your answers if you have time.

After each test, check your answers. On the questions you missed, be sure you understand why you missed them. Did you misread the question (tests can use tricky wording)? Did you forget the information? Or was it something you hadn't learned? Go back and study any shaky areas that the practice tests reveal.

Taking these tests not only helps with your grade, but also aids in combating test anxiety. If you're already used to the test conditions, you're less likely to worry about it, and working through tests until you're scoring well gives you a confidence boost. Go through the practice tests until you feel comfortable, and then you can go into the test knowing that you're ready for it.

Test Tips

On test day, you should be confident, knowing that you've prepared well and are ready to answer the questions. But aside from preparation, there are several test day strategies you can employ to maximize your performance.

First, as stated before, get a good night's sleep the night before the test (and for several nights before that, if possible). Go into the test with a fresh, alert mind rather than staying up late to study.

Try not to change too much about your normal routine on the day of the test. It's important to eat a nutritious breakfast, but if you normally don't eat breakfast at all, consider eating just a protein bar. If you're a coffee drinker, go ahead and have your normal coffee. Just make sure you time it so that the caffeine doesn't wear off right in the middle of your test. Avoid sugary beverages, and drink enough water to stay hydrated but not so much that you need a restroom break 10 minutes into the test. If your test isn't first thing in the morning, consider going for a walk or doing a light workout before the test to get your blood flowing.

Allow yourself enough time to get ready, and leave for the test with plenty of time to spare so you won't have the anxiety of scrambling to arrive in time. Another reason to be early is to select a good seat. It's helpful to sit away from doors and windows, which can be distracting. Find a good seat, get out your supplies, and settle your mind before the test begins.

When the test begins, start by going over the instructions carefully, even if you already know what to expect. Make sure you avoid any careless mistakes by following the directions.

Then begin working through the questions, pacing yourself as you've practiced. If you're not sure on an answer, don't spend too much time on it, and don't let it shake your confidence. Either skip it and come back later, or eliminate as many wrong answers as possible and guess among the remaining ones. Don't dwell on these questions as you continue—put them out of your mind and focus on what lies ahead.

Be sure to read all of the answer choices, even if you're sure the first one is the right answer. Sometimes you'll find a better one if you keep reading. But don't second-guess yourself if you do immediately know the answer. Your gut instinct is usually right. Don't let test anxiety rob you of the information you know.

If you have time at the end of the test (and if the test format allows), go back and review your answers. Be cautious about changing any, since your first instinct tends to be correct, but make sure you didn't misread any of the questions or accidentally mark the wrong answer choice. Look over any you skipped and make an educated guess.

At the end, leave the test feeling confident. You've done your best, so don't waste time worrying about your performance or wishing you could change anything. Instead, celebrate the successful completion of this test. And finally, use this test to learn how to deal with anxiety even better next time.

Review Video: Test Anxiety
Visit mometrix.com/academy and enter code: 100340

Important Qualification

Not all anxiety is created equal. If your test anxiety is causing major issues in your life beyond the classroom or testing center, or if you are experiencing troubling physical symptoms related to your anxiety, it may be a sign of a serious physiological or psychological condition. If this sounds like your situation, we strongly encourage you to seek professional help.

Online Resources

Due to our efforts to try to keep this book to a manageable length, we've created a link that will give you access to all of your online resources:

mometrix.com/resources719/flg5sci

It's Your Moment, Let's Celebrate It!

Share your story @mometrixtestpreparation